LIGHT SONGS WE BREATHE

By William Serle

Light Songs We Breathe

Dedicated to my beautiful children

Kim, Bill, Jeff, and Kris.

Just hoping I've been an okay dad.

Photo by Melissa Serle

ABOUT THE TITLE

Joyce Kilmer's work has entertained me since early school days. His poem, **Poets** conveys a deep meaning, speaking directly to my *inner poet*.

POETS

Vain is the **chiming of forgotten bells**
That the **wind sways** *above a ruined shrine.*
Vainer his voice in whom no longer dwells
Hunger that craves immortal Bread and Wine.

Light songs we breathe *that perish with our breath*
Out of our lips that have not kissed the rod.
They shall not live who have not tasted death.
They only sing who are struck dumb by God.

From *Trees and other Poems*
By Joyce Kilmer – 1914

BOOKS BY BILL

Works by Bill Serle include four novels, three biographies, four books of essays and poetry, and a screenplay. They are available on Amazon and Kindle, except as noted.

FICTION

Stealing Ali
Hunter I
Hunter II
Hunter III
Hunter Trilogy
Fred's Gold (A screenplay) *

NON-FICTION

*Bill's Journey**
*Edna's Love Letters**
*Gammy**
Grandfather Uber
Chiming of Forgotten Bells
Swaying in the Wind
Light Songs We Breathe

*Available at <u>billserle.com.</u>

TABLE OF CONTENTS

Light Songs We Breathe

LIGHT SONGS
WE BREATHE

THE MOST USEFUL
And Important Thing I've Ever Done

Yes, children and grandchildren are high on the list. But so are careers in the Coast Guard, in banking, medical administration, food service and publishing. There were many good moments.

Surprisingly, one of the most useful and important things this earthly visitor ever did was to sit and write a memoir in the early years of this century – *Bill's Journey*.

The book was intended to celebrate life. Photographs and art illuminate the many good days. The art gave a glow of happiness and made the stories more personal and authentic.

At first, it was a digital document posted on a website at billserle.net. It was of some amusement to my computer-savvy grandchildren. Then it took a back place to Stealing Ali, the novel co-authored with my dear wife. Daisy, based on the true story about the international kidnapping of our daughter – my brilliant stepdaughter, Kris. That book is now a part of our family's history.

Bill's Journey caught the attention of **Jenifer Lee**, a young Englishwoman in the United Kingdom. She was searching the internet to find her husband's long-disappeared grandfather, John Joyce. She was on maternity leave, so she had some time on her hands for the project.

She sent an email asking me to put her in touch with our friend, Peter Joyce, who was mentioned in the autobiography. Jennifer's email set off a compelling chain of events.

Englishman Peter Joyce was in the book because Daisy and I made trips with him and his wife Norma to destinations, including month-long journeys to Thailand, Costa Rica, Spain, and Mexico. The travels were just part of the autobiography.

It turned out that our friend Peter's name was *John Peter Joyce*. He divorced and emigrated to Canada, not realizing that his ex-wife was pregnant.

His life involved further emigration to the United States and then to Mexico, where he resided until his recent death.

The condensed version of the story is that Peter was happily joined to a hitherto unknown daughter, a grandson, and a great-grandson because of *Bill's Journey*. His lost family subsequently held reunions in England, Greece, and Mexico. This beautiful family reconnection seemed monumental to me.

As a friend once wrote, 'A great teacher's words echo down the hallways, but a writer's words echo down the generations.'

A little bit more about *Bill's Journey* – after a few years as an Internet document, we printed 30 copies to distribute to friends and family

If I were doing it now, I'd use a company called kdp.Amazon to enable me to create a digital book on Kindle and a paperback book that could sell on Amazon and which would be suitable for libraries.

I swore off book 'making' after publishing *Swaying in the Wind* because I thought there'd be a few more sales. It was a labor of love. But a new body of poetry, essays, and memoirs have piled up that need a resting place other than on top of the little-used paper shredder.

The working title was *This is Not a Book*. It is a sort of junk drawer of little gems I can't bear to toss aside. I'm just neatening the office and my mind – and passing the time. Everyone likes the title *Light Songs We Sing* better

Please browse or read a few pages. Perhaps you'll find a precious stone to put in your pocket.

Bill

Flagler Beach, Florida

I think that I shall never see
A poem lovely as a tree

POETRY

This includes previously published poems
to make this a rather compete collection of
the ditties Bill has penned over the years.

ABOUT POETRY

This is a slightly paraphrased excerpt from Greg Olear's
political blog. (gregolear@substack.com)
He rang my bell.

Poetry is about language. The best poetry manages to capture the passion, emotion, love, lust, joy, and sorrow, of the poet, and to transfer those feelings – like an incantation – a magic spell.

It does this through by word choice, phrasing, meter, and rhyme (or not rhyme), by having our understanding of the poem enhanced with every reading.

The best poems manage to access the sheathed tuning fork of my soul and make it ring out. The best poets do this years, decades, centuries after they are no longer alive. It is literary magic.

THE PLAIN PAGE

A plain page
Challenges
To gain thoughts sage
My pen to lay.

Words can be a maze.
Thoughts lost in the haze
May bubble to the top
And spill out as I jot.

Persistence pays
For ideas rise
To bring a smile
At thoughts worthwhile.

So, as you wend 'long your way
And I have my little say,
I crave to make your day
As aft you gang aglay.

This is why
I'll always try
To find the way
To have a say.

On this blank page
My words are laid
The tempting pane
Not plain I said.

My friend Ed Rahn helped me with the last stanza

SAILAWAY

Summer's warm breath
Grazed my cheek as I lay
Beneath Sun's genial ray.

Old pocket-yacht heeled away
From Southwind's urgent flirt
With White Sails billowing skirt.

My tired eyes were lightly laced,
As Mind drifted to the Peaceful Place.
My Mate's hand mastered eager Helm,

Eyes upon the Buoy nigh,
She is all set to come about
With a "Ready…Helm alee!," shout.

Life was straightaway under control,
Away from Stress of workaday Troll,
And n'eer a phone to snatch me

Away from my nappy face.
And now, five decades on,
I recall that happy place.

Many moons far away in time
But not forgotten by my mind
As happy thoughts do kindly find
Old Fart, some lame, a tiddly blind.

Thus, a thankful smile,
As I pace the final mile with mirth
On this appealing pile
Called *Señor Earth*.

THE SPEED OF LIFE

Popped out one fine day
To say, "What the hey…"
Things were going good unfurled
"I'm not ready for *this* world…"

Woke in the morning
Cried like a baby
Hoping for A. Juice but
Then got warm Milk – maybe?…

Up in early morning
School bell's a'ringing
Mom begins a'yelling,
"Yellow bus's a'coming…"

Got up late this morning
Body's gotten so tall,
Feeling blue at the U
My standing is so small…

Damn alarm is ringing
TV's raging and singing.
Boss watch's clock like a hawk
So, I have no time to gawk…

Nowadays I'm the boss.
No room for goof-offs Hoss,
Deadwood has gotta roll
Or I will take the fall…

Gold watch is plated
My car is dated
Now it's time to meditate
And I need to medicate…

Bye fer now.
Holy Cow!
We are gone so soon,
It's not even noon…

MY PATH
Looking Back and Cheering

***** Out of the gate *****

Hey you! Tiny new person. All-promising,

Baby with human traits to be imprinted.

Learning many "No-no's," and "Good boy's,"
every single day

To become a self-actuated soul in every way.

***** 10 *****

Oh, the joy of our youth's surging vim

Springing from those wellsprings deep within

Demanding to be let out and shout.

Step out, step out, you, shy boy, Step out.

***** 20 *****

Step out, step out, you silly shy boy.

It is time to claim your birth-earned

Domicile on this fair shining sphere.

Come on boy let's go now. Don't you fear.

***** 30 *****

Happiness-seeking man doing his best

For his dear family and community

In a most serious race, but lagging behind,

Doubts assailing his ordinary and troubled
mind.

***** 40 *****

Change is a'coming

Don't hold back.

Pull hard man! Don't fear the dark.

You're on a new lark.

***** 50 *****

New work. New friends

Wild mountain ranges

And rivers dancing in the sun.

They call for working

Just for fun.

***** 60 *****

Finally, there is peace inside

As the challenges are met

and new higher goals be set.

Racing again with joyful energy

Toward a happier synergy.

*** **70** ***

The earth is big
The water's fine.
Change of pace again
Moving toward the
blessed end of chaos.

*** **80** ***

As octogenarianism is realized
Wisdom arrives with time to meditate.
Then with slow steps and careful gaits
We find a surer path to meet our fates
Each and every step leads back to that gate.

CLASS CLOWN

Alas, it is Tuesday
And I have nothing writ
For my Writing workshop.
They'll think I'm a dumb plop.

A poem? Ah yes indeed
That's what I really need
To show them that I do care
And am brave enough to dare.

Pen to paper with head down.
Squeezing a few words and frowns.
Will this be good enough
To prove I'm up to snff?

Yes, of course. This poem rhymes
And it is certainly mine.
But the deep human mind
May be missing you'll find.

There is no hint of soul
Or mention of high goal.
So, must I hang my head down
And fear that I'm the class clown?

But, wait! There may be more
Just before I out the door.
Better yet I promise, next time,
To polish every silly line.

LE MEMOIRE IN PROGRESS

Plop!

I was born in a state of ignorance and learned my place in the world from my family and neighbor children. I wasn't ever high on the totem pole of life.

Craack!

My education was sporadic but quickened after years of university Then OJT when I learned how to move the World along..

Smiley face!

I created my own family out of wisps of dreams. Now they've spread out across continents. Many are gone.

Swish!

It moved along so fast. I have a gold watch. I Paid for it myself. A pension or two and a new place on the totem pole.

Phoosh!

I'm getting old – downright elderly. My cane helps me get around, but I still don't exercise enough. Hair's gone, grips problematic and…

Last call!

Getting close to closing time. I'd better place my order now – perhaps a month on the French Riviera? How about a visit to the polar continent?

What?

Help the less fortunate? Of course. At every opportunity. There, but for the gr-c- of G-d go I. You know what I m--n.

Light Songs We Breathe

Plop in the morn
Milk at noon
Loved my naps on
Silk and down.

Up in dark a.m. hour
Cream of oats or corn.
Galoshes for m' feets
And pencils in m' bag.

Three clock's so long
Games on the block
With pals until we hear
The song of dinner bell.

Birth ~ Then too much school
K thru 12 ~ then OJT
Slow moving clock ~ Last call

Gotta go to the U
And get it quick
Cause it seemed
To make me sick.

Work never quits
Blame never stops,
We gotta make more
Or fall on swords

Magic twilight
Pastels every hue
So, the end is near
Does heaven appear?

T-BIRDS
AND INSCRUTABLE HONEYBEES

To be mildly suitable
A man must be awfully kind,
And not strive for unreachable
Merits lodged in the female's mind.

Women on the other hand
Do quite well to understand
He-humans are not unteachable,
And give hints, not Inscrutable,

Of their innermost desires
Whilst earnest suitors 'kick their tires,'
Just like chumps at car dealerships
Stroke their auto fantastaships.

Please don't cover your ears
And give in to your silly fears.
Things will always work out right
Whether or not we strive and fight.

The final score's not ours to see.
Actuaries of Heavenly scope
Will let us know what's to be
Whilst we wring our hands and hope.

The earth, the stars and constellations
Are just giant hallucinations.
This is, as it should be, of course,
And won't be changed by any force.

WILLY AT THE BEACH

The sun was hot as anything,
I the coolest dude that spring.

My wool swimsuit was cute fer sure.
I might have been almost four.

Mommy said, "My oh my, that's so fine."
But I pranced around, my feets on fire.

So's I sticks my toes into the water
And found a crab I shouldn't oughter.

So's I splashed out to the sandy beach
To see my sweet, pinched, swollen feet.

But there weren't nutten to see
So's I swam, swam, swam back out to sea.

Nevermore to fear that something hides
In the deep and swirling watersides.

GRAYS
HOME COOKED F

LITTLE WILLY

A week at the Jersey shore was my first remembered introduction to the beach. I ran into the water and before I knew what happened, a crab bit my big toe. It hung on and I high kicked it off. It hurt and I screamed out of the water and refused all entreaties to go back in – for the entire week. I pouted on the beach blanket and built sandcastles at the water's edge.

At the end of the week, as the car was being packed and the kids were jamming inside for the ride back to New York, I, on my own, decided to go back into the water.

Wow! It was great! I flat-out refused to leave waves and get into the car. I was finally hooked out and left our part of the beach crying.

BILLY AND THE MONSTER

Daddy, "I can spell energy,"
Billy declared when he was three.
My boy's face was very grave.
"Do tell," I said while I did shave.

"It's N – R – G, isn't that right?
I told you he was very bright.
So, then I struggled not to laugh.
Yes! He was right! At least by half.

We wrestle with the written word,
And confuse it with what we heard.
Picture books help a lot you know.
Signs and such teach how words flow.

~~§~~

To a seafood restaurant we did go,
After the motion picture show.
Little Billy studied the menu
At that special seafood venue.

For great decisions must be made
'Bout things we eat and cannot trade;
About our evening dining pleasure,
That all-important meal of leisure.

First deliberation, with aplomb,
Then in cahoots with proudest, Mom,
Billy announced, loud and clear,
"Yes, I'll have the monster here."

THROUGHPUT
Random thoughts on a stormy day

Equal or unequal brain momentum.
Where fast moving infinity ball hits ball at rest –
Then stop while resting ball takes off like crazy.
I need a hit on the head.

Too many thoughts out. Process slows.
I must find great books to hold
If my life as a writer shall proceed
Must make time to think and read.

Words in. Words out. Fiction read
All lies? Some tales true?
Young minds keen to understand
Artful books, that only hint at life, may

Not be worth paper carved from trees.
Look up. Take time to think before you leap
Upon a notion only then it false to see,
Are *my* tales like chiming bells above forgotten
shrines?

Ideas in. They float about.
Notions came screaming out.
Sometimes even history books miss the truth.
Have to think that some tales were base on a
kind of reality.

Stories told. Belief unfolds.
Who-da thunk? Young minds mold.
Then learned the author's awful story
Is based upon another's glory.

What is true and what is fake?
What is trash and what has value?
What a rush to understand
That all is good in the proper hand.

***

Truth is a moving target and
There are many truths, Grasshopper.

THAT CONSCIOUS LOYALTY

I've analyzed every aspect
Of my mind and now suspect
That thoughts I have held so dear
Are chaos underlain with mere

Wisps of joyful tomfoolery.
Matters, mixed simply and coolly,
Without understanding of life
And full of stupid fear and strife.

My consciousness is annoying time,
Between naps, that imposes lines
Of thoughts into my weary head,
Snafuing a love affair with bed.

Yet deep within my heart I heed
A certain loyalty to feed
My country and my dearest tribe…
Unless you'd consider a bribe?

Please humor me my dearest friends
Whilst I ponder 'bout my ends.
Will I amass gold upon this loam,
Or buy tickets to the Lofty Dome?

WAH, WAH WAH, WAH!

Wah, wah, wah, wah!
My knees are dumb
My feet'r numb
And oh, my hips do smart.

Ha, ha, ha, ha!
My mind is sharp.
My eyes are keen…
And I heard that!

~~~

Ah, ah, ah, ah.
We take deep breaths
And feel the breezes
And even see de swaying treezes.

Up, up, up, up
and away, we hasten.
Work needs to be done
And time's awastin.'

Rain, rain, go away
My flowers're drowning,
The hay's way too wet,
N' my roof's holey yet.
~~~

Light Songs We Breathe

Yum, yum, yum, yum!
Our bellys are full
Our naps're at hand
Oh ain't life grand.

Amen, amen, Brother.
Jesus had it right
Forgive ye one another
And love with all your might.

~~~

Sigh, sigh, don't sigh,
Nothings Perfect
All is good
And for the best.

Yearn, yearn, yearn, yearn
Trust that we will earn
A bit of rest if we
Learn to pass the test.
~~~

ENDLESS SATISFACTION

What cannot be bought or sold?
Way more dear than pots of gold,
Much better than being king,
So sweet my soul taketh wing.

Life's my daily miracle
With taste, touch, sound and smell.
I, a merely earthbound slug,
Cast my eye to skies above,

Trapped there by those ticking clocks.
Vainly looking up above
To see birds in thrilling flight.
Whilst I try with all my might

To reach out in praise devine
For the many blessings mine.
I, undeserving and flaw'd,
Feel the universe's draw.

How much more might soaring gull
Place value to his winged days as
He drifts high o'er the wavy sea
And targets me, as on the lea

I, defenseless and grounded plod,
Where planted firmly on the sod.
In cosmic views, my weary, wandering mind
Seeks satisfaction of immortal kind.

RESOLUTE SQUIGGLES

My mind is so completely blank,
Mine muse a troublesome old crank.
So many words have lately come
As fired from the wordsmith's gun.

I can scarcely sit to think
Much less use paper and ink
To help me imagine fun jogs
O'er green hills, fields and distant bogs.

I thank goodness for those swell prompts
My friends gave me at Tuesday's romp.
So, on this Monday morning fine
As I stare at that empty line

The first words seem merely squiggles,
As my mind wiggles and giggles
Through poetry's literary swamps
And as my resolute finger stomps

On my keyboard's cloudy connection
To computational invention
In which I'm very likely lost.
I suppose this page must be tossed.

Newest prompts, "squiggles" and "Resolute"
Resist any sensible compute.
Perhaps, maybe, some stauncher writers
Of stern bearing, much better fighters,

Could make a sensible essay
One worthy of their weakened pay,
An ode for ages just ahead
Beyond which I'll never tread.

GUILT AND SHAME

My sister ruled the house
And resented me, the louse.
She was taller, blond, and cute
While I was ugly as a newt.

Yes, they thought her very smart,
She got straight A's and didn't fart.
I was a noisy, noisome brat
On whom she would always rat.

The guilt has haunted me
Since I was gnat-high to a flea.
My sins were piled awful high
When evil sister drew nigh.

Shame followed everywhere
From kindergarten, yes, I swear.
But then I grew some, by Jove,
And sibling warfare turned to love.

Remorse for mean traps laid,
For tender nerves frayed,
For that stolen pizza slice
And other things, not so nice.

Sweet redemption became mine
When kindness began to shine.
We forgave each and every sin
And now we are the best of kin.

Happiness came on quiet feet,
Whilst ripening souls became more sweet.
Aging out's not a fast curve,
So, I got what I deserve.

On the same page
for many years.

SISSY SLIP

Sissy slip
Broke her hip
Surgeons used stainless screws
Now we get the best of news.

Short and sweet hospital stay
Full recovery one soon day
Lots of cool rehab stuff
She'll be more than up-to-snuff

But she's a girl of 86
Her hubby's 91 and his slip
Caused a really broken hip
His repair was not so swift

There are lessons for old folk.
Balance and strength are no joke
Extend your years of health
Avoid much loss of wealth.

SNAPPY BONES"

The work piles up,
The brain slows down,
Yet when the phone rings
My whole body sings.

Another job, I'm thinking,
More folks I'll be adding
"To the mighty client list
To bill and stroke and kibbitz.

So, I'm happy nuff,
At eight-ought-years plus,
To merit just a bit of fuss.
New friendships are another must.

Cold cash comes to the till.
And more! There'll be stories still
To amaze my kin.
And yet, deep within,

My hope's for wealth of years,
To enjoy health, my dears.
It drives me to exercise
Snappy bones to gain that prize.

COMFORT ZONE

Old age is a mess
But I must confess
This seniority is not so bad.
My ideas are older than my dad.

Too shy then, when I was much younger,
Ugliest sib and slowest runner.
Just stepping out of mine comfort zone
Caused me to squirm, to moan and groan

Much of mine good fortune on this earth
Is owed to the great public speaking coach
Who helped me to escape mine doubt.
He routed fears and gave me clout

To stand, to question, to manage
And lead in business and in civic affairs.
No matter the size of the crowd.
"Seek ye truth in thought, be bold,
And the words will surely flow."

Light Songs We *Breathe*

Now from a lofty age, there's no doubt
That it's awfully good to step out
And away from the old easy sectors
Because good things hide in other vectors.

A new problem was lack of chums
To while away the time in fun.
So, I promoted a poker club
And now enjoy many card-shark buds.

Oops, I forgot to say, at eighty and a click,
I had enough conviction to kick
Off a wee airport transportation establishment
Providing services for nearby inhabitants.

MY OLD PAL

Just saw Huey
Good friend of mine.
The day well spent,
I slept just fine.

We brash Brooklyn boys
Bonded from the start.
Lots of energy for life in any direction
But geography broke our connection

Had not seen one another
Yes, more'n sixty-six years last,
Sitting together, old timers now,
Felt like just a few yesterdays passed.

The spark still in his eyes,
Strong comradely love, true friend,
Good humor, dare I say it,
We'll recall our days 'til the end.

Hail Huey!
T'was good, Eh?
Please, old pal, do not wait for me,
I'll See you again some other fine day.

Commemorating a visit with Huey Develin after many years. He was in an upstate New York Senior care facility. We were boyhood best friends in Brooklyn. Huey passed away in the spring of 2021 at the age of 84.

APPRENTICE YEARS

Remembering untoward incidents,
When I've sinned against my fellow men,
Forgetting to be just and fair,
Makes me blush from toes to hair.

There have been many times
When I, feeling unkind,
Downright dishonest, even mean
When wise behavior, it would seem,

Could better serve and ease the pain
Of awful moments when, again,
I was unable to stay the path
And be the man Momma tried to craft.

Teaching moments fade to the past
As nature matures me and, at last,
Piling high apprentice nods,
I will join God's Angel Squads.

~ ~ ~

Make amends my many friends
Ere we reach our several ends.
Go back down thine evil roads
To help brotherman with his loads.

A MOROS RECIPE

Cook those black beans and boil the white rice.
They're different but, when cooked together, so
nice.
The dish is 'Moros' – short for
Cristianos Y Moros
Black and white, Moors and Christians, *negros
y blancos.*

Rice, a staff of life, tastes good enough
But is much better when mixed with beans
Enough to give rich flavor
And mouth textures to savor.

Even better, as you chew and swallow,
The divine slither of sweet green peppers
And onions sweated on the stove so hot
It married the ingredients in the pot.

~~~

People can mix just so,
Each one brings something to
The work and art of the world
Whether it be high or low.

All work is important.
The soft hand that rocks the cradle
Is not less than the hard hand that
Breaks the earth in construction.
~~~

Pyramids would not be possible
Without the planner and the laborer.
The boss with the whip is just mush
Without a simple grunt to push
The blocks up into the sky.

~~~

Abundance is more possible when people
Cooperate as often as they compete.
So, let's celebrate in common cause
And work like demons to avoid wars.

Look around and what do you see?
Are they working just like you and me?
Happy faces will always make me smile
I relate to their happiness all the while.

Can we celebrate our differences
Without indulging mean thoughts and hate?
Kwanzaa, Hanukah, Ramadan and Christmas
Could elevate earthly peace to Heavenly state.
~~~

MIAMI JOY

Among the joys of our many years in Miami was the beautiful Cuban cuisine the refugees brought with them.

Early days for Daisy, my beautiful Cuban wife, and I, were graced with beautiful celebratory meals at her many relatives' homes. Roast succulent pig, *porco frito, platinos masduros, moros,* black beans and rice, and so much more.

I love the Cuban food as much as any type of food I've ever encountered. It is well-seasoned but not hot or peppery. Savory with foods, like yucca and plantains, that most Americans do not know.

Platinos look like large bananas but are not eaten uncooked. They are left to get very ripe, peeled, sliced and fried to a golden, honey-brown in olive oil. A little crisp on the outside and sugary deliciousness on the inside. The Cubans call this *masduros*.

When black beans are cooked with rice the dish is called *moros*. I ordered moros at a Cuban restaurant one fine Miami afternoon. Seated at the table were Daisy's Uncle Caesar, Daisy and a few friends.

Tio Caesar, a fun-loving man, leaned toward me and said, "Beel, do you know why we call eet *moros*?"

I confessed my ignorance and he told me, "Eet ees called *moros* because dot ees short for *Cristiananos* and *Moros*. White and black people," he winked.

I had an 'aha' moment as I recalled the terrible history of Spain. Hundreds of years of conflicts between Christians and non-Christians culminating in 1492 when the Moros were defeated and kicked out of Spain. Jews were kicked out in 1493. Ethnic cleansing is a terrible thing. Even today, scholars shiver when they recall the horrors of the Spanish Inquisition.

This conversation with *Tio* has percolated in the back of my mind for many years and finally finished as the poem on the preceding page. Enjoy!

* * *

P.S. Would you like the recipe for *masduros*?

Okay.

Buy a number of the ripest plantains you can find at Publix. Put them in a paper bag under your sink. Wait a week and take a peek. They will look a little riper – even black – but not too soft.

Put them under the sink again and leave them alone until the skin is black and the insides seem soft to the touch.

Wait! Don't throw them out. Peel them to find the soft slimy fruit inside. Slice the softness on the diagonal and fry the thick slices in hot, extra virgin olive oil. Both sides.

Be careful not to burn them. They turn brown suddenly. Be prepared for "ohs" and "ahs" at the dinner table.

SCOREKEEPER

My scribbly lines,
Are often kind,
But never,
Hardly ever

Smart and sassy.
Not too classy, say,
Just blasé
Calls to play.

Father time
Friend of mine,
Keeping score
And much more.

The birthdays mount,
Many to count –
Too many now.
So, holy cow!

When will it end?
Never to send
My simple
Thoughts again.

FATHER TIME

Father Time please stay away,
      Come again another day.
      Too much work too much play
      Makes Bill happy and gay.

But I must rest, sleep and nod
      As I prep for each new job.
      Magic carpet to distant airports
      Whisking clients to their sports.

Chew that pencil, tote those verbs,
      Adjectives and blurbs.
      Craft more books, essays and poems,
      Tote the trash and answer phones.

Off I go to the meet
      To see my friends so sweet
      Then a rest, time to recharge
      My batteries small and large.

Bye and bye I'll answer the call
      And so must we all.
      Did the best that I could
      And tried to be kind and good.

EVERCHANGING LIGHT

Evening sun aglistens on
The Spanish moss clad oaks,
Their black trunks agnarling
To Frame the golden hour
Before old Sun sets so red.

It's time to sit and ponder
About fortunes allotted
To this denizen of the world.
Hark Now – not to rhyme ain't no crime
But not to reason is mindly treason.

As temps rise from cool to warm
Light changes from soft to sharp
Whilst the day passes us by.
Mornings are seen through misty air
Still much laden with midnight's dew.

Evening's breeze is dry and clear.
Yes. Quiet time, this end of day.
Birds a'settling, a time to ease.
Could my mind rest so well

Light Songs We *Breathe*

As news pundits tell
Of dastardly enemies
Plotting harm to our well-favored land?
Mindset moves from 'do' to 'done' as old
Age bring clarity to mind.
Life's temperature changes while
Old Time marinates experiences.

Another day in the bank
To be savored with interest.
Some are good – some worrisome.
I thank the Power for
Her bounteous gifts of
Time and consciousness.

Tomorrow – who knows?
Next week – too far.
Next year. Nevermore.
A million or a billion
Out of mind and reach. Evermore.

TO BLOG OR NOT TO BLOG?
THAT IS THE QUESTION

Do you yearn to share
What you learned
Ere schoolhouse Burned?

Blog away Comrade.
Sling awful truths taught
We'uns too-young fought.

Turn on Laptop, Desktop, Pad
Kern those sentences so great.
Compel them to reverberate.

Earn the right to bend ears and eyes.
Don't be a shroom in need of bull,
Say, "Sprinkle me with answers full."

Give me the key, unlock my cage.
Help me turn happy dreams
Into schemes within my means.

Help tame my rages
With strong blog pages
Born of brains and wit.

I long to grow,
To be the one to know
And unashamed to show.

SNOW ANGEL

Whispering Snow decorates dapper Earth
In a flowing alabaster wrapper.

As Snow falls, we hope for beauty
Everlasting and cool repose.
Clothing our world in purest white.
Snow. Whispering. Tingling cold nose.

Snow-time slows, thought flows,
Seeking Truth.
And, so cool and light,
In snow I just might

Sigh, tumble back,
And a winged
Cherub make for
Your sweet delight.

CAN'T RANT

T'was early fall early fall
When I made the call
That left me sad
And feeling bad.

The spooky voice said,
"First Bank of North Trent.
Please press one if you
Are calling about payment,

Press two if you are past due.
And three if you are calling
About something else and
Four if you are not sure or can't
Remember that Time in September."

With hope in my pit
I pressed zero for operator.
Said the voice in a snit.
"That is not a valid response!"

"Press five if you want
To hear this menu again."
I cried, "Foul," and kicked poor
Radiator, my favorite dog,

Who was only humping my leg,
Because he knew not to beg.
"Oh please, just give me the Refunds,
Discounts and Cancellations
Departments, or perhaps
Just stop some allotments."
I screeched.

Remember, "Hi, First Bank.
How can I help you?"
Instead of, "Due to higher
Than normal call volume, wait..."

Raise your hand if you've ever dated an
operator.
Sing praise if an issue resolved
was as easy as apple pie.
Say, have you ever dated an apple π?

Hours misspent as many a minute
Went out of my bank of days
Listening to, "This call will be
Recorded" for uses

Not yet decided or glibly disclosed.
Give me a break! I'm not disposed
To go that place of pain
Where policies are proposed!

I cannot wait
Cause soon or late
Artificial Intelligence
will get overdue come-uppence,

And humans will say,
"Hi. How can I help you?"
Oh, oooh. Oh, oh, oh, happy days.
It cannot come too soon.

DEAR AMERICA

Oh yes, our Dear America's first rate
So, let's proclaim it already great!
Our favored land's laws must be fair to all
So that we can stand up proudly and tall.

Since we are human – not perfect
There is some room for improvement.
Flaws in laws can be away sent
To help all in happiness' bent.

Ignore today's worn-out bodies and souls
And see tomorrow's minds take energy
And mightily grow as do the tiny seeds,
To monumental ideas to match our needs.

All peoples have high potential,
Not just today's ruling class.
Look ahead and you'll see a Mount Rushmore
sculpted
with Asian, red, black and Latino heads.

To Hot Hell with that stupid wall!
There's room enough here for us all
On warm meadows reaching to the sea.
China's teeming millions, newly freed from
want,
Have created a powerhouse to vaunt.

Two heads are better than one.
Hundreds of millions are better yet.
Let us do the math as the Warmheartedlies
dream
About the greatest meet of minds
Earth has ever seen.

IN THE WACKO WEEDS

Oh, where did the waiter go?
Service here is gettin' slow.
Now I'm in the weeds n'sad.
Why oh why do I feel bad?

Gone to Mexico a long time ago

And where did my gardener go?
Now I'm watchin' the weeds grow,
Barrow's gone – I've got no hoe.
I feel sore and weak-ee-oo.

Gone to Mexico a long time ago

Where did my friend Pepé go?
He's been my best amigo.
All alone and feeling blue,
Oh Pepéito, I miss you.

Gone to Mexico a long time ago

Now my brother's gone away, I'm
feeling alone and gray. Time's
passing, years seem to fly
As I wait for bye and bye.

Gone to Mexico a long time ago
Mom and dad and Uncle Bert

Light Songs We Breathe

Aunt Maria, Cousin Gert,
I wish that you all were here
Working hard for you and me.

Gone to Mexico a long time ago

All gone 'way to Mexico
Where living is sweet and low.
I'm agoing soon to see
Monterey and Puerto V.

I'm Gone to Mexico a long, long time ago

****

I wrote this little ditty some time ago and published it on billserle.com and in Swaying in the Wind as a coda to an essay asserting the value of immigration – even undocumented immigration.

My piece decried the harsh and unwelcoming treatment of harrowed humans at our borders. As of now, the situation is awful.

Perhaps, some-soon-day, our national Immigration and Customs Enforcement agency will welcome refuge seekers and help them on their way instead of keeping them in makeshift, concrete jails.

In fact, if had my way, we would transfer the Immigration Enforcement functions of ICE to the U.S. Department of Health and Human Services and put Enforcement elsewhere.

DON'T BE ONE OF THEM

It seems to me that most humans are reasonable, loving, civic-minded sorts that pose no danger to each other. Yet, in human history, vile, large-scale episodes of ethnic cleansing and prejudice towards certain groups break out, which stain all humanity with the evil brush.

This limited and somewhat scrambled list only hints at what I am referring to:

BC
Hebrew people Enslaved by Egyptians

Romans
Roman Empire

The Modern era

Western Europeans
The Crusades
Middle Ages
Eastern Europe

Holy Roman Empire
Empire building
Late Middle Ages
Middle east and Europe

Turks (Byzantine Empire)
Empire building

Christian Spain
1490
Moors Expulsion

1492
Jews expelled

Spain
Inquisition and expulsion

Western Europe
Colonial empires

America (and many others)
Slavery
Native Americans

United States
Indian wars and Removal

Nazi Germany
The Holocaust

United States
Regime Changes

20th century

Muslims
Balkans
Ethnic Cleansing

Italy
Ethnic Cleansing
Ethopia

Turkey
Armenians
Ethnic Cleansing

21st Century – The Beat Goes On

Isis / Muslim Fanatics
Ethnic Cleansing

Russia invades Ukraine

~~~

While the Evil beat goes on, we should remember that life is good for more of humanity each year.

The percentage people in abject poverty is now smaller than ever before.

One theory is that as smart phones and other technology spreads, prosperity will follow.

I loved the book *ABUNDENCE The Future is Better than you Think* by Peter Diamandis and Steven Kotler. It nudged my world view in a good direction.
~~~

DELIBERATE MINIMAL IMPACT

I should'a listened to my sis
When she said I'd meet a miss
Who'd give me a precious kiss,
And then offer me her fist!

Then I looked around at work
'til the gang called me a Jerk.
But always the perfect twerp
I began to creep and lurk.

Then Night Sky sported Full Moon
And, as I heard Dreamy Tune,
Along came a girl named June
And we married pretty soon

We never, ever got Mad.
And then I became A Dad.
So, don't be too awful Sad
Because I the best life had.

I can't say with these minimal Words,
That oftentimes seem like flying Turds
Dropped on me by deliberate birds
As hinted in old odes from Kurds.

This little poem was inspired by a joke-essay I wrote for a
writing workshop. It was fun to cob together.

AN ARROW FROM AFAR
Dedicated to my favorite teacher,
Taylor Larrimore

A low-energy morn,
Whilst I sit all forlorn.
I needed something to write.
Had to finish it last night!

Sad to say, and to my dismay,
I did not do it yesterday.

Browsing through old email
My ashes wan and pale,
I found something to inspire
From an old and trusted friend.

That letter struck hot sparks in me
Like a flint arrow hitting stone.
And yes, there was tinder
Waiting for that cinder.

Bright hot sparks aflame in my soul.
A story began to unfold.
The friend from fifty years afore
Had sent a missive kind and pure.

***

Today is my workshop – yes, it's at one,
And I have absolutely nothing done.
Still quite low on vitality's peak
Into my phone I began to speak.

Out came quaint thoughts about
"The most useful and important
Thing I have ever done."
In a trice, an essay was finished by one.

The well-intended essay was ready to share
Thanks to that awfully smart phone over there,
That converts speech into text, and to my
supercomputer.
What will they think of next?

Thank you old archer,
My fellow marcher.
Long may your words
Reach out to teach.

Photo of Taylor
taken from a
website.

Here is the email correspondence that inspired the poem. I found my Effective Speaking teacher some 50 years after I took his class to present him with an essay named *My Favorite Teacher*. He was, in fact, my favorite teacher.

RE: friends forever
Sun, Mar 1, 2015 1:05 pm
To: billserle@aol.com

Hi Bill:

I am very glad to hear from you – so close yet so far.

I am very pleased to learn that your speech experience helped you nail the CG officer job with eventual Commander status! I know you were a credit to the service.

I have done many things, but I think that teaching "effective speaking" was the most useful and important thing I ever did. You are my best example.

It appears you are a follower of Thoreau. His book, Walden, changed my life towards "simplicity." It is my tag line when I post on www.bogleheads.org. (put "Taylor" in the search box).

If you come down to Miami for the weekend, I'd love to take you and your wife sailboat racing—which Taffy and I do every Saturday (weather permitting) for about 3 hours.

Best wishes.
Taylor

From: Taylor Larimore
<taylor.larimore@comcast.net>
Subject: friends forever

Hi Bill:

I'm still living in Miami and, until 2 weeks ago, very active and healthy. I just had a melanoma cancer operation on my face which seems to be healing OK, but I'll probably scare the kids.
Your beautiful story of how I helped you learn to speak effectively is the best therapy I could ever receive.

I live at 1541 ****** Ave, Miami, next door to where I was raised. I hope you are living nearby so we might get together. I see we are both authors.

Taylor.

From: bill serle [mailto:billserle@aol.com]
Sent: Sunday, March 01, 2015, 11:07 AM
To: taylor.larimore@comcast.net
Subject: Re: friends forever
Hello my beautiful friend. Wish you a speedy recovery
No plans to visit Miami although we live in Rockledge near Cocoa Beach. Miami is the big bad city now, even though I sojourned there for over 30 years. Maybe…one of these days...
Do you ever get up this way?
All the best,

Bill

Bill here again. I was so happy to have reached out to Taylor. It made my day too.

BILL

I wanna tell you a story
'Bout a man named Bill
Cause if I don't tell ya
Nobody will.

There'll be some glory
And a smatter of pain
It's a little gory with
A morsel of shame

It may be the story
Will clear up my rep.
Cause I'm trying to
Erase every misstep.

So, sit back and smile
And let me entertain you
For a very short while.

THE BIG QUESTION

As I slide through my twilight years
And earthly time's end draws near,
What to seek? How to labor? Time grows late.
Which I ask, selfish welfare or mankind's fate?

My voice in these wilderness years
May not be heard by needy peers
Who can't shed attitudes cast in stone
Against Humanity's endless cry and moan.

"Set my people free," they shout,
"To care and forge happiness out
Of abundant golden days on earth
And claim the rights all have earned at birth.

"Set us free to follow our path
To find heaven's gated wrath,
Free to dream of heavenly grace
And free to claim our rightful place."

~~~

I have a dream of brotherhood,
Of equal rights well understood
For all who sojourn on this patch
Are under the Lord's kindly watch.
~~~

We know that many together are strong,
All are needed to push the load along
And one alone cannot last long
And sing the universal song.

One's a solo, two's a duo. Many are a
symphony.
So, bang drummer, let fly the flute,
we'll launch into the sky
Our lofty songs, and our grandiose noise,
Hymns to fill cloudy canyons and starry voids.

OH, TO BE ME

Why is it good to be me?
Every day is a blessing.
Many in the memory bank
My jar of days is first rank.

My joints do creek.
My legs do speak
Of neuropathy
In my mind some weak.

Old Failure's no longer a fear
I don't fret 'bout what to wear.
My hair has sadly gone away
And my gait's a bit asway.

Though age be nighing ninety
I think of my life kindly.
Each new hour finds me singing
Of plans to celebrate living

On this planet fair
With sweet flowing air,
Sunlight clear, strong and bright
With birds in lofty flight.

It's good to be me
And I guarantee
When Time says, "goodbye"
I'll happily lie

In sweet repose
to rest at last
With no more woes
When my jar overflows.

GET DOWN AT WILLY'S

Me heart was muchly brightened
By de show around me chair.
De gale struck me upturned face
And me life was very fair.

De dianthus and de daisies were aswaying in
de breeze,
Dey was Dancing like crazy In de shadows of
de trees.
Fat Palm he was shimmying, Slender Fronds
dey was shaking.
Big Windy sighed real loud 'n blew Ol' Sun
behind a cloud.

D' evening is now arrive on dis day of de bash.
Night sky she much alive Whilst Planter
Moon'n stars clash.

We'll have a doo again tonight,
Be ready for a jolly scene.
I'll get me down in delight
Ovah big love for mah Queen.

The *Get Down at Willy's* lines came to me as I luxuriated in the hot tub under the twin palms that bracketed our hot tub patio.

This was a private place that prompted lazy thought and deep love for life – a place of comfort and hope. It begged for fun and frolic too.

The spa was screened from view by substantial palm trees, high board fences and a screened patio. On the fourth side, just seven feet away, were the sliding doors leading to our master bedroom and bath. Sweet.

Our modest Rockledge, Florida home was beautiful, inside and out. The new Flagler Beach home is elegant, but I miss my secluded hot tub."

AWFUL ODE TO POLITICALLY INCORRECT FRUITS AND NUTS

Nuts are salty and hard to understand.
Fruits dress better than Nuts. Fancy that.
I, on the other hand, have five fingers,
Two rings and a small red thumb tat.
I am both a fruit and a nut!
And a nutty fruit at that.
I am silly Billy bar.
So thar!

BLESSINGS OF ABUNDANT TIME
GETTING OUT OF THE AIRPORT TRANSPORTATION BIZ

Blessings of abundant time
Will, again, soon be mine.

Busy work, but just for money?
Not for me – not even funny.

I do intend to be a crafty wordsmith
Alert for sentences ending with 'with.'

And not be the silly guy who then starts
sentences with 'And.'
Nor he-who-forgets to put in a period at
the end

I mean to end too-long, run-on
sentences
That could be stand-alone paragraph
lengthisis.

And don't even get me started on page-
long paragraphs.
Just remember that he who laughs last,
laughs, laughs.

Airport transportation, no more for me –
don't fret. I quit!
'Cause I want to do the publisher bit.

TUESDAY – 11:00 O'CLOCK

11:00

My Muse has fled
My brain is dead

Need to write something new
But ideas are very few.

Fell on my head
"ER," they said

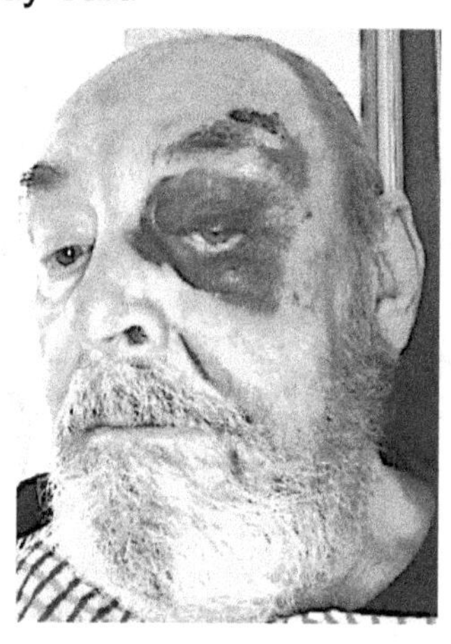

Slowed me a bit
Refused to sit

Hours in Med limbo
Watching clock so slow

Two weeks have flit
along
Whistling my first-rate
song

11:20

Holy cowski!
What nowski?

CRAZY WINDS OF CHANGE

"My name is Bill and I'm a writer," was my lead.

"Hi Bill," the group chanted in unison." They understood addiction.

"I want to tell you a story about childhood in Brooklyn, being a student at the universities, Coast Guard basic training, bank worker, medical administrator, restaurant owner, Coast Guard Commander, shift manager, cook, server, newspaper publisher, sous chef, novelist and the head of my family…"

The audience drifted away before I got to Brooklyn. I should have found a shorter subject – or maybe – write a book…

Everything changes. When I think about the members of my family, all those gone and those yet remaining, their lives have been a kaleidoscope of heavy change. Employment, work, marriage, parenthood, life, death, and even climate meander us away from planned paths.

It seems to me that the way to cope is to be ready to bloom wherever you're planted by the winds of change. If you fall, get up again. Keep your spirits high. Be optimistic.

The 'Pursuit of Happiness' is a universal passion. We chase her while we work to earn and keep our place on the planet.

CRAZY WINDS

Ol' Southwind blowing strong and steady,
Warms and smooths the way ahead.
Family, friends, shelter, food and hay
Are yours 'til it blows t'other way.

Eastwind brings the rain and flood
So ye must prepare to dam the flow
Or be swept away far down the stream
To places 'bout which ye only dream.

Westwind's dry and crops will fail.
Prices rise, good jobs are rare,
Ye must put forth your utmost best,
Hold strong to deal with every test.

Northwind is strong and gusty
Driving us with thoughts so lusty.
Fight and claw to stay on earth,
Find peace, kindness, love and mirth.

Start over when you trip and Fall
Grin, persevere then stand up tall.
Keep smiling there's a dream indeed
Though your path cannot be guaranteed.

Writing these words led me to think about my father, Bill Senior, and his path from life to death. He left a wonderful legacy as a man overflowing with good will to all, love of family, good cheer and courage. He lived four score and four years. He came from a broken home in the days when divorce was uncommon. He struggled with change, moving from the great city of Brooklyn, New York to Hicksville. Think of what those names could entail.

Bill Senior thrived, studied hard and was working as a stationary engineer for the New York City subway electric power generating plant when he met and married Edna, my mother, in 1930.

America's entry into World War II led him to train for and become a marine engineer in about 1942. He served as chief engineer by the end of the war and stayed onboard ships until 1954, when he lost his job due to an oil spill.

Edna, always a hard-working, high-ranking secretary, fell victim to a stroke in 1949. She passed away in 1958. Despite many hardships throughout her life, she was always a kind, loving and trusting person.

So, back to Dad… 1958 was a rough year for Dad. He lost his wife. His business went under, and he wound up in jail. He fell hard, got up and worked his way back up. He never lost his ability to look ahead with optimism. He found peace, love, kindness, prosperity, and mirth, despite the crazy winds of change that kept blowing him off course.

Read *Bill's Journey*, my autobiography, for more details. It's free at billserle.com.

TOUGH LIFE

Meat, bone, gristle in plain fact
Tough as hell is where they're at.
But grind them up a bit by gosh,
And you may not need to toss.

Or you could find a bit'a fat
Fry it juicy in a vat,
You got it made so don't snit
Eat that crispy bacon bit.

Or boil it in water, hot.
Wait some tics and watch the clock,
Salt first, then let it simmer.
When it dings, then it's dinner.

Cover, simmer another hour
Pretty soon, it's no more sour.
Don't complain you have a tough life
You will not even need a knife.

Gristle and meat turn soft and sweet
After they simmer for a treat.
Please smile and cook it tender
It'll end well for you my friend

Talk with me 'bout stinky onions.
Cook 'em soft and pretty soon…
Okay Cookie, now we're neighbors.
We'll making happy flavors.

Close to the end? Never curse.
Not to worry, it gets worse.
Always simmer in the pot
Let it rest, then serve it hot.

Dontcha complain. Enough. Enough!
Go off muttering, "Too damn tough."
Complain, complain – sounds like noise,
What a neck-pain girls and boys.

Carrots, turnips, very nice
Add some honey, salt and spice.
Heap some peas upon our earth,
Then we'll smile and share the mirth.

THE NATURAL DISASTER

I don't have much acquaintance with natural disasters. Yet I feel that I am a part of the natural disaster that is the human experience. I'd like to share some word couplings and progressions that may resonate with your own experience e.g.

Born – Die
New – Old
Joy – Sorrow
Greetings – Farewell
Yesterday – Today
Tomorrow – Beyond
Sooner – Later
Forever – Never
Healthy – Sick
Boy – Girl
Friend – Neighbor.
Married – Divorced
Near – Far
Countryman – Foreigner
Earthling – Alien
Rich – Poor
Child – Stranger
Friend – Enemy
Found – Lost
Confusion – Certainty

Right – Wrong
Rise – Fall
Try – Fail
Try – Try – Try – Again
Dark – Light
Gray – Color
Soft – Hard
Offend – Forgive
Hurt – Help
Master – Servant
Kind – Cruel
Sweet – Sour
Happy – Sad

This is the nature of our disaster, i.e., human life.

To be alive is part of a system that often feels like a descent from organization into chaos. Yet what joy we find along the way!

WALK BRAVELY

Judge not evilness lest ye be judged,
But dare assume good to ease your day.
Walk bravely. Hold your head so proud,
You own the town and all surrounds.

Assume all men are Godly til
Ye be shown a fair denial.
Your ancestors fought to make it so,
They, the heroes, who before us go

To say the magic words, we love,
All men are created by G-d above
As brothers and sisters to savor
The fruits of our sweet earth's labor.

TERRIBLE TIMES TABLE

TIMES ONE

Maria wept. She cried. She wailed.
Her mother has gone away.
"Where am I now?
 "Where am I going? Must I stay?"

 TIMES TEN

My casita was so warm.
This place is so cold.
No one to talk to.
No one to hold.

  TIMES ONE HUNDRED

I had a sister and a brother.
I cannot touch these new niños.
Such strange food to know
We stand in line, just so.

   TIMES ONE THOUSAND

"Who are these people? What do they want?
                "Why am I here?
                "Will Mama come back?
                "Where is my Papa Dear?

TIMES THIRTY THOUSAND

I wake in the dark and fear.
We have to go now. Far or near?
Where can I sit. There is no room.
Where am I going? Home or doom.

TIMES ONE- HUNDRED THOUSAND

Voices meld and rise
In song sad with cries.
My heart's askew
What can I do?

Jesus wept!

MILE-A-MINUTE MAN

My minutes are stashed in a box
Made from all the days of my life.
The number actually in it
Will be known when I reach my limit.

I get to spend them as I will
On matters great and small
And hope not to waste them
Doing who knows what for all

I cannot buy more minutes and
I should not sell mine for gold
They can't be borrowed or loaned
Nor metered, saved, or sold.

So, all care must be taken
To use them just for right.
Once spent they won't be returned,
Only passed along or spurned.

If you have a plan for life,
And it's about time that ya do,
It must include a minute budget
To recall and savor every nugget.

~~~
~~~

You and I have many regrets
and want time back to redirect
toward worthier ends
and to try to make amends.

Are my best days gone now?
Fading in a rearview mirror,
Never to be recalled by
Some power perched on high?

Minutes deferred too long degrade,
And young time is worth more than old
The Formula, Time X Energy (T)(E)
Might equal (=) great accomplishments I
believe.

Look up now, is that a dust devil
Or an angel glowing in the sun?
Do you cross fingers to improve your story
Or hope for beneficent endless glory?

MEMOIRS

A CELEBRATION
OF FLORIDA, MY NOW-HOME STATE

Paraphrasing Wikipedia, Florida wetlands generally include swamps, marshes, bay heads, bogs, cypress domes and strands, sloughs, wet prairies, riverine swamps and marshes, hydric seepage slopes, tidal marshes, and similar areas.

To my eye and heart, I love the lake shores, rivers, waterways, and beaches as well.

I often drive along our oceanfront highways and marvel at the constant energy and beauty of the ocean.

Patrols of pelicans are seen almost every time. They fly in formations from just a few birds to patrols of a dozen or more. They seem to hug the

shoreline to take advantage of the updrafts, conserving energy as they stretch their wings and bodies to an ideal aerodynamic shape.

I confess to using Quinton Ellison's beautiful photograph without permission. (Tink. – If you catch me, I'll be glad to publish a new version with proper permissions, if possible, and, if you want, I'll give you any ill-gotten gains.)

My daily neighborhood wanderings take me through the tidal wetlands of Bulow Creek. The cover photo is a sight I see many times a month. The scenic byways in Flagler County are my highways. The views, like the pelicans and the image below, delight me every time I venture out.

MY FIRST PIZZA

I remember my first pizza. The year was 1945. I was an unruly seven-year-old boy who woke early to discover a funny shaped box on the dining room table where my parents had enjoyed a poker night with Aunt Betty and Uncle Dick Wilhelm.

Janice, my evil older sister was in dreamland on the Castro Convertible sofa as I tiptoed past, and everyone else, Nanna and Mom and Dad were sleeping elsewhere in our two-bedroom Brooklyn apartment. I had no idea about what might be in the box and when I identified it as edible, I made an executive decision to sample the goodness. Boy was it good – I could not stop eating and consumed all four slices.

There was a little bit of trouble with my sister Janice when she woke. She claimed she had dibs and was outraged at my sin. Mom was annoyed that the shouting woke her early but, by and large, the reward was worth the penalties. And I learned that the food was called 'pizza.'

Since then, most everybody in America has enjoyed the most famous Italian export. Prior to the end of World War Two, pizza was unknown but GIs returning from war in Italy gave it a start. Here's a bit of my 75-year pizza history.

• Naples. Italy – We Expected great pies here and we were not disappointed. Rustic, deep brown, crisp crusts, well done, super tasty. We ate pizza at the same crowded restaurants every day for a week and made friends with the waiters.

• Nowhereville, France. – A little lost, and a lot hungry, somewhere between Paris and Normandy, we discovered a little restaurant, with no clients at an odd time in the afternoon. We made some noise and the owner grudgingly agreed to sell us pizza and beers. We were worried because we were out of euros and there was no ATM in this little burg. Communications were difficult. When we finally made our dilemma clear to the owner/chef, he said, in French, don't worry. *"Pas de problem. Si vous avoir plastique, je avoir pizza."* Yea MasterCard! Was it good? Yes! Very brown on the bottom. Not too much (or too little) cheese and sauce.

• New York City – Original port of entry for the Italian treat. Little pizza joints everywhere. Our Flatbush neighborhood had several within an easy walk. (New Yorkers don't have cars.) Brooklyn was and still is a Mecca for pizza lovers. We even have New York Pizzerias in Flagler Beach and Palm Coast, Florida.

• Rome, Italy – We had the joy of sharing a couple of slices at the Trevi Fountain whose famous fountain sculptures are now more than 250-years-old and the plaza is usually covered with tourists. But we were first there in winter; February 1993. We shared the place only with pigeons. We've been back several times but have never been able to enjoy the Trevi the way it was on that first, fine February day. It's too popular.

• Corfu, Greece – Daisy and I tarried here for almost two weeks and had many wonderful meals at some fine restaurants. But the only actual food I recall is pizza. Seems that these pies involved feta cheese and black olives. The weather was perfect. Most of the time we ate outdoors in the shade or in the evenings under the moon and stars.

• Sarandé, Albania – Eating by the seaside in this tiny resort town with grandniece Meg Johnson and her boyfriend Nate – we ate a lot of pizza because that was the specialty of the local joints. I believe that it was just as good as Brooklyn. But the crusts were not round and even. They were a bit more rustic – just the way I liked them. We passed three wonderful days there and the only thing I remember eating is the free breakfasts at the hotel Brilliance and the waterfront pizzas.

• Sydney, Australia – We spent three lovely days here and, you guessed it – pizza in the shadows of the Opera House and the Sydney Harbor Bridge. Ditto The Pacific Islands, Hawaii, Canada, Alaska and even in the shadow of the Space Needle.

• San Juan, Puerto Rico – Daisy fell flat on her face while stepping up a curb in front of tiny hole-in-the-wall restaurant on our first day! Thankfully she wasn't injured by the unexpected trip. Passers-by and restaurant staff rushed to her assistance and lifted her to her feet. The helpers could not have been nicer or more caring. This is a beautiful example of strangers in a strange land coming to the aid of a person in need. Daisy claimed that the circular delights we had there were the best ever. And she should know. We went back for lunch there the next day too and she did not fall.

Mmmmmn!
Those Italians.
By the way. Sam's club
makes a great pizza
too. We're having one
for din-din tonight.

Serendipity. Lately we've been making our own pizzas made with refrigerated dough from the grocery store and a variety of toppings. How about caramelized onions, gorgonzola cheese and thin sliced pears on top. Not very Italian but Mm mm mm!

STICKBALL

My Brooklyn was centered around Martense Street where our apartment was located. We had the first floor of the building, which was in the middle of the block. Most of the buildings were two and three-stories tall, and they created a canyon in which children could play safely. The families were mostly Irish-Catholic.

The canyon walls were brown and ocher with the exception of, what we called the 'New Red Apartment Building,' which rose to a towering six stories and had an elevator.

Maple and sycamore trees lined the entire block on both sides, arching over the roadway. The street had cars parked on both sides with scarcely ever in a vacant parking space. New Yorkers didn't use their cars much. My family kept our Nash Rambler in a garage some three long blocks away.

When I first ventured out of my apartment, I fell into the company of nine and ten-year-old boys. I was tall for my age so, even though I was only seven-and-one-half years old, I fit in pretty well.

The stick ball game that I'm going to describe took place in the middle of the street. We used a red

rubber Spaulding ball. The bat was a broomstick from some unsuspecting-mom's cleaning closet. Home plate would be a convenient sewer. Bases were chalked on the street.

Teams were determined by a schoolyard pick with the boys in a circle as two leaders picked the teams. The leaders would take turns choosing until each side had maybe three or four boys. That would be enough to man the bases with one outfielder.

Traffic was at a minimum and when the occasional car came, we would shout "CAR," and clear the roadway for a few moments.

The sound of a stick hitting a round rubber Spaulding ball was a unique 'plop-plunk-flap' that remains still in my middle ear somewhere. I even remember the way a new Spaulding smelled.

Because the older boys had better-developed skills, I was always the last one chosen and usually relegated to third base where very little action would occur. I was not a good catcher or batter, and an awkward runner. I was happy to be chosen – last.

You see, not every child on the street participated. Girls never.

Peter Robins, a Jewish boy who lived on a second-floor apartment near our preferred game area, sometimes looked through the window, but I think he was too busy with his studies to participate. Once in a while we'd go to his house on a rainy day and play Monopoly.

Edward Talley never played with the kids on the street although he was in my PS 246 third grade class. I think he was smart but his handwriting and drawing skills were zero and he had no athletic abilities or interest. His mom kept him indoors in the big red apartment building. Little Patrick Leone was too young and small for us.

Wilbur Smith and the Hartley boys, at the end of the street near Bedford Avenue, never played with us, but they were believed to be good athletes, and probably good guys. Just standoffish.

The shouting in the streets and the *thwuft* of the red rubber ball being hit with the stick remain firmly in my mind. We experienced an occasional whiff of car and bus exhaust. The grinding of the trolley cars on Church Avenue, the birds in the trees and the joy, the absolute joy, of playing with my friends, remain in implanted in my soul – a kind of anchor in my lifelong journey through time.

I still remember the names and qualities of each child in my inner circle:

Frankie Hennigen – 12 – an older boy; tall, trim and athletic.

Huey Develin – 10 – Hefty. You noticed when Huey bumped into you when rounding the bases.

Billy Whalen – 9 – Young, like me. Slim and very well liked.

Bobby O'Connor – 11 – Wonderful kid. Nice manners and very athletic.

Billy (Fiendish) Ferry – 10 – Always a little awkward but fun to hang out with.

Vinny DiJoya – 11 – Short but a terrific hitter and base runner.

Eddie Ford – 10 – Serious about stickball and everything in his life.

Johnny McNicholl – 12 – Irish – just off the boat. Good at running and catching. Not tall but a bit of a firebrand.

Billy Serle – 9 –Tall enough but awkward. Acts like a damn nine-year old.

Sixty-five years flew by since I last saw my friends. We'd lost touch. I've met up with John McNicoll, Eddie Ford and Huey Develin in recent years. I'll send Johnny and Huey a copy of this and post it on my blog. (billserle.com)

What a blessing to remember and to be remembered.

JOHNNY JUMP JUMP

The photo on the facing page was taken from a Facebook group post. It evoked a powerful emotional response deep in my chest. We called this rough-house activity 'Johnny Jump-Jump.'

One boy acts as base and the horse team, could be three or more boys, bends over and links against the base, as shown, heads between the legs to form a sturdy horse.

The rider team pies on top, one at a time, as rough as possible, and wriggles around trying to knock the horse over!

No one ever got hurt in my experience. I don't know why because we were trying hard.

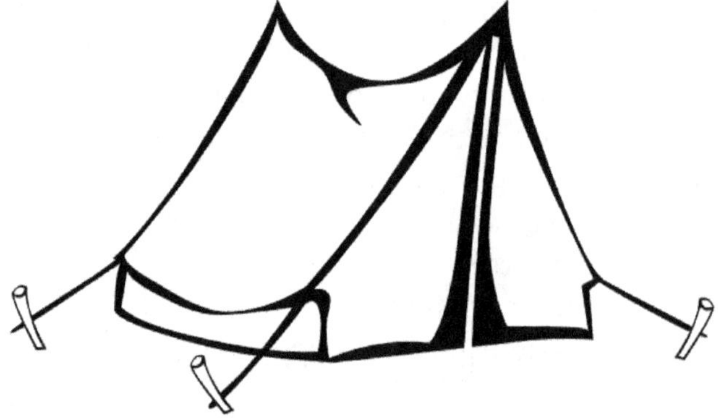

PLANNING AHEAD

There came a time when a young man's *fancy* turns to camping. Thus, it was in the fall of 1950 that five of my friends and I sat on the stoop of an apartment building in Brooklyn and decided that it would be a grand adventure to pack some camp gear into duffle bags and backpacks and take the subway from Flatbush to Manhattan's George Washington Bridge. "We can hike across to Fort Lee, New Jersey and have a camping weekend on the high bluffs overlooking the Hudson River," was the final decision.

We were ex-Boy Scouts and had had a little experience. *What could go wrong?*

It was a cold fall. "Let's dress warmly, bring lots of matches and plenty of food. Each of us will take whatever he needs, and we'll use Huey's six-man tent."

Present were Huey Develin, Eddie Ford, Frankie Hennigan, Bobby O'Conner, Billy 'Fiendish' Ferry, and me.

I, 12-years-old, the youngest member of the expedition, decided to take my ice skates. They were a size ten, and I was outgrowing them before they ever touched ice. It was freezing out and I envisioned an icy pond, deep in the woods.

I don't remember what the other lads, 14 and 15 years old, brought. I'm sure they made better choices. I do remember that we were all heavily burdened. We must have been a sight as we put our nickels into the subway toll turnstiles. We had to make several underground route-changes, and then hike along unfamiliar neighborhood streets. We were already a little travel weary when we finally caught sight of the GW Bridge.

The bridge crossing went off without a hitch. It was about a one-mile hike, but it seemed longer because of our heavy bags.

Then, in Fort Lee, New Jersey we discovered that the cliffside park area was still some distance away. Luckily, we stumbled across a bus to take us to our desired camping area and loaded our gear into the suitcase storage under the bus.

It was getting a little dark when we reached our destination. "Holy Crap!" shouted Fiendish as our transport roared away. "We left our food bag on the bus!"

What to do?

We decided to split up. Fiendish and Frankie would grab the next bus and try to chase down the food bag. The rest of us would hike into the woods and make camp.

My nose was red, and my toes were cold. I was very happy when we got a fire going and began to sort our gear out. We were all weary. Darkness had arrived. Rest was near.

Suddenly, out of the woods, an amplified voice startled us. "THIS IS THE FORT LEE POLICE DEPARTMENT." Only then did we notice the flashing red light on top of a nearby police car. "PUT OUT THAT FIRE NOW AND LEAVE THE AREA. NO CAMPING IS ALLOWED HERE."

We obeyed. Worried that our retrieve-the-food task force would have a hard time finding us, we didn't move too far – just deeper into the woods, hoping that the police would not see our new fire. We four campers huddled around the fire.

It must have been ten or eleven p.m. when our successful two-man-food-bag team found us. We feasted on baked beans – right out of the can.

It was too dark, and we were too tired to put up the tent. So, we decided to sleep in the open near the ever-dwindling fire.

My sleeping bag was a summer-weight affair. Before I could get settled Eddie announced, "I forgot to pack a blanket. Billy, can I climb into that bag with you and share?"

"Heck no, Eddie. This is a one-man bag and it's too small – even for me."

Eddie, desperate, climbed in anyway. We passed a long, uncomfortable, and wintry night, struggling for space. We woke, early in the morning, covered by a two-inch snow fall. We breakfasted on some cold soup from cans and decided to go back to Brooklyn.

Pack. Trudge. Bus. Hike. Subway. Subway. Subway. Walk. Home at last!

Lessons learned:

- Never, ever, pack ice skates for a camping trip.
- Make a list of essentials for each boy to carry.
- Check the weather reports.
- Leave home early in the morning so you can see to put the tent up.

I long ago forgave Eddie for making my night uncomfortable. *Hmmm? Perhaps he kept me from freezing.*

TIME IN A BOTTLE
Je Maintiendrai

Our lifetime supply of days is limited.

Like the jellybeans in a big jar – we are challenged to guess the number of days our *lifejars* contain. But there is no prize for guessing correctly.

How do we make the best use of our time on this planet?

Do we want all the jellybeans to be the same color and flavor? For me, I like variety and little surprises as well as the tried and trusted.

My life has had quite a variety of experiences. Most often I was pushed by a quarter century of *lousybossosis* and *lackafunditus*. I overcame and became my own boss only to learn that I was also too harsh and demanding. Midlife, I discovered, that one could fix *lackafunditus* by changing venues and simplifying needs.

I was born and raised in temperate-zone city-life in Brooklyn, New York. In my mid-teens I had agrarian experiences in Farmingdale, New York. I moved to sub-tropical Miami and then fled, 30 years later, to abide in the rural mountains of Western North Carolina for two decades.

So, my *Life-jar* is filled with varied locales and experiences that often result in interesting tales to tell the grandchildren. Sometimes I was the boss, sometimes I was the slave, and sometimes both.

There have been so many failures – yours truly sometimes forget the triumphs that luck and persistence brought me. Graduation from the University of Miami occurred after my firstborn came into the world. I retired from the Coast Guard Reserve with the rank of commander after 30 years of service. I married a strong and beautiful woman – we just celebrated our 47th anniversary.

Our four children and fourteen grandchildren are doing well. I sense persistence and commitment in their lives as well. Retirement has been bountiful. Luck, *Health*, *Wealth* and even *Happiness* have often visited our home.

I've been lucky, but also think that stubbornness in my pursuit of goals has paid off. When I attended Hofstra College, now a university, I was given a little pin with the motto *Je Maintiendrai*. This is French and means "I stand steadfast" or "I shall maintain." To me, it means "I shall persevere." I believe that any success I've enjoyed has involved persistence.

For example, Daisy and I decided to open a sandwich shop in an office park in Southwest Miami. We had limited funds and were told by the facility manager that we could not lease. Their zoning would not permit a restaurant.

I wouldn't take that for an answer and convinced the owner to sign a lease conditioned on my successful attempt to change the property's zoning. I filed the required appeal forms and appeared in front of a hostile zoning commission to plead the case.

Months later, the zoning was changed, and the property owner was so impressed that he became a limited partner in a second restaurant we later opened in North Fort Lauderdale.

Another instance of persistence was my eight-year stint as an enlisted man in the Coast Guard Reserve before my, long-awaited, university graduation made me eligible for commissioning as an officer.

If I were telling my grandchildren this story, I might finish with, *"Je Maintiendrai."*

MISTER IN BETWEEN

I viewed life through negative lenses for many years. A second child behind a brilliant and lovable older sibling is not a comfortable position. She took prizes for goodness and light. Little Billy caught the blame for all the messes and was too often reminded of his lowly position in life.

Outside my home in Flatbush, Brooklyn, New York, I played with older children who had better-developed athletic skills because I was tall for my age. Thus, I grew to regard myself as unathletic.

As a freshman high school student, I fell under bad influences and became a truant. That resulted in a difficult year made worse by the fact that Mom, my caregiver, was suffering the effects of the stroke – an illness that ultimately took her life, some years later, at the age of 52.

My work life was punctuated by the smell of manure, mean bosses, unsteady employers, divorce, kidnapping, failing businesses, burdensome debt, and such.

Lingering whisps of life haunt my dreams at night. They tend to be full of personal problems that I cannot solve. In one recurring nightmare, I've been called back to active duty in the Coast Guard. I need to report to my new commander but cannot find the right bits and pieces of attire to be appropriately garbed. In the armed services, being in proper uniform, with the badges and insignias displayed in the correct positions is important. In my sleep fantasies I cannot even find matching socks. And my hat is a disaster. You get the point ¬ – I'm reliving some negative elements I experienced in real life.

Thankfully, fears are gone now. I define myself by counting my successes: Beautiful children creating plentiful and accomplished grandchildren. A successful career as a Coast Guard Reserve commander, a banker, newspaper publisher, medical administrator, author, literary publisher, and several small businesses. I was a serial entrepreneur. I now enjoy living arrangements that are suitable, beautiful, and paid for.

My finances are in alignment with my situation in life and that enhances my happiness.

So! Why bring all of this up? I do it to assure readers who may be experiencing negative times and complex problems that things will change in time and get better. And, when you begin to view all situations with a positive viewpoint and, in your rearview mirror, just interesting pages in your story, your life can improve, as did mine,

Meaningful friendships with interesting people and time to grow emotionally and spiritually is a great blessing. Wiser spending and investing bring peace of mind. And, as the beautiful Johnny Mercer song advised:

You've got to accentuate the positive
Latch on to the affirmative
Eliminate the negative
Don't mess with Mister In-Between
You've got to accentuate the positive
Latch on to the affirmative
Eliminate the negative
Don't mess with Mister In-Between

FREE LUNCH - NOT

I am a little greedy, so I jumped right in when I got an offer of a $500.00 cash bonus just for opening a bank account with Bank of America. The main string attached to the deal was that I had to make direct deposits of at least $10,000 within a three-month period, from payroll earnings, pensions and the like. Easy peasy. Right?

So, I checked with Chase Bank, who had lured me with a similar offer a decade, or so, ago, to see if they'd make an effort to keep me on their books. I spoke with a branch manager who didn't seem to care. So, after getting the go-ahead from my dear wife, Daisy, I began the process. There was a little procedure to deal with, but we now have accounts with Bank of America. All I had to do then was to get our two pensions and Social Security to start the direct deposits.

Then I pondered and realized that I should contact the several credit accounts, insurance companies and other concerns that we pay by direct charge to our bank account so that our bills will be paid as they come due.

I made a list of all those trusted companies who are paid automatically, and the real fun began. The list had 23 names and I began to contact them, one at a time, using my internet provider and, when necessary, the telephone.

Some companies were easy. **Great!**

Some were challenging. **Grrr!**

Web addresses. Telephone numbers. Login credentials. Passwords. Challenge questions. Account numbers. Bank Routing numbers. Confusing instructions. Poor connections. Long waits and call-backs. Age fatigue. And my never-ending, but human, tendency to make clerical errors have been my lot this week.

Most often I got things right. Many errors were correctable with earnest effort and patience. Only one issue remains to be solved and I'm home free! I had to work for my five-hundred-dollar reward. I'd guess I put less than eight hours, so I had a fair hourly return. Ask me in six months and I may be able to tell you that it was worth the effort.

I take comfort in the fact that much of the rigamarole is for my benefit, to insure the privacy and security of my financial affairs. Safety is important.

I'm hoping that the drive-through tellers at Bank of America have lollipops to share with clients – I hope they're free!

<div align="center">~~~</div>

Did I get the $500.00 bonus?

Yes. It came, March 25th, after several long-wait phone calls to the bank's 800 number and two visits to the local branch.

I had to work for my bonus and have yet to get a lollipop...

PERSPECTIVE

I grew up in the Flatbush area of Brooklyn, New York. For a seven year stretch our domicile was a two-bedroom apartment that housed my parents, Edna and Bill Senior, my paternal grandmother, Nana and my older sister, Janice, and me.

It was always a big treat to visit my Aunt Belle and Uncle Bert Helmer in their home in nearby Saint Albans, Queens. The Helmers had a swell house filled with wonderful cooking aromas and hearty laughter. The house was a kind of French Provençal style with a huge backyard and a veggie garden.

I realize now that it was a tiny house. When we sat in the living room, we filled it up. But it was warm and happy. Now addicted to Home and *Garden TV*, I would now want to knock down walls and build an addition to open things up and make the house larger. But I doubt if it could be made kinder or happier.

The Helmer family of five included my older cousins Joan and Dorothy and my grandmother, Gammy, whose real name was Annie Conover. My folks, my sister and, sometimes, Nana would load into the family car and go a'visiting. So, there would be up to ten people sitting in the Helmer's living room or bellied up to the dining table.

Uncle Bert, my parents warned me, was a stickler for good manners. They told me that if I *ever* failed to use the butter knife when lathering popovers or mashed potatoes with the yellow gold, Uncle Bert would get out of his chair and take the butter to the kitchen and wash it.

I was always careful but, *wink wink, hee hee,* I doubted that he could get to the kitchen from his chair because the dining room was so crowded.

Sadly, I now have only two links to the Helmer family. My departed cousin Dorothy's two living sons. The rest of the clan are gone.

One of my keenest memories is hanging out with Uncle Bert in his big barnlike shed. "Billy," he said, opening a very large paper bag, "Stick your nose in here and tell me what you think."

The brown fuzzy stuff in the bag didn't look like much, so I bent over and inhaled. *SHIT!* I thought.

"What's it doing in that bag Uncle Bert?" I was about to throw up.

He floored me with the answer. "It's sheep shit. I use it to grow cabbages and carrots." I thought he was joking, just like when he tricked me into sniffing the foul contents of the fertilizer sack. I never quite trusted him again.

A better perspective kicked in about 20 years ago when I retired.

I have lived in many homes and apartment. Some of them have been smaller and some grander than that house in Saint Albans, New York. I now know that my happiness was never in proportion to the size of my home or my wallet.

And another thing – my whole adult working life seemed polluted with mean bosses, surly coworkers, unsteady and even failing employers, as well as my own mistakes and misadventures.

The fears and the smell of manure are gone, and I now regard the untidy process as the adventure of life on earth. I try to remember my several successes as well as my failures and seek peace within. I forgive those who have trespassed on my pursuit of happiness and hope that they too can forgive me.

My final thoughts are that the kindness, good-spirited fun, and humor in my family were channeled through Gammy and Nana. I underappreciated them my whole life until now.

Thank you, you two lovely women, Nanna and Gammy, for the magnificent inheritance!

Janice, Edna, Bill Senior, Billy. This was taken *circa* 1942 when I was about five years old. In St. Albans, Jamica, New York.

MY MUSIC LIFE

Some of my earliest and strongest memories are poetry, prayer, and music. This essay is a meditation celebrating the interplay of these elements as they frolic through my mind and soul whilst I journey through this life. I'll use the decades to put it in order.

1940s – When I was almost four-years old, in 1941, I was ill with a fever and lay abed, attended by my grandmother Nana, Mom, and my big sister. When they turned down the light Nana taught me to say,

"Now I lay me down to sleep
And pray the Lord my soul to keep.
And, If I die before I wake,
I pray the Lord my soul to take."

The rhyme was fun, I thought, but the meaning of the words scared me. *I must be really sick*, I thought. Brrrr.

From that same time in my life, I was first allowed to go alone to the corner of our block and back. I pushed that envelope and soon turned the corner and came upon big tough kids, probably seven or eight years of age, who taught me songs like:

Whistle while you work,
Hitler is a jerk,
Mussolini is a meany and
Tojo is a twerp.

I loved it and remember it to this day – even taught it to my youngest kids.

My all-time favorite from that age, and at that corner of the block, was:

> Pepsi Cola hits the spot
> First you vomit then you fôt.
> Only a nickel, twice as rich,
> Make you feel like a son of a bitch.

Tee, hee hee – naughty words, I thought.

Also, in those tender years, I fell under the spell of poetry and music that still echoes in my heart and soul:

> *The Old Lamplighter…*
> *The Roaches and The Bedbugs Were Having*
>   *a Game Of Ball…*
> *Eenie, Meanie, Miney, Moe…*
> Robert Louis Stevenson.
> E. B. White
> *The 23rd Psalm.*
> *Rock Of Ages.*
> *Onward Christian Soldiers.*
> Any Christmas Carol.
> *The Peer Gyntt Suite.*
> *Ghost Riders in The Sky.*

I would listen to records on our Philco combination radio/record player, returning to the same songs over and over again, to memorize the words.

Early 1950s – in rough order, here are some verses and songs I felt. Pause for a half sec on each one. I reckon I've overlooked many good ones. See if these ring a bell:

You Ain't Nothing but a Hound Dog.
Rudolph the Red Nosed Reindeer
Far Away Places
Smoke Gets in Your Eyes.

In the 1950s I progressed through high school and college. Elvis hooked us as we watched him on the Ed Sullivan Show.

Late 1950s – I'll call this my Dark Period. I was a starving student at Hofstra College in the fall of 1955. I had no money, no radio, and no record player. I got left behind on these earlier days of rock and roll.

I did like Chopin's piano music. This was free in Hofstra's music library. I drowsed away hours in the little booths listening to classical albums, opera and so forth. **I should have been looking for a job as my savings disappeared and Dad's ability to support me dwindled.**

There was an exception to my blackout. I was able to see my first Broadway show in early 1958 while on a break from Coast Guard basic training – 'Standing Room Only,' in my dress blues uniform with one stripe on my arm, of course. Robert Preston starred in *The Music Man,* and I loved it…. *Seventy-four trombones led the big parade…*

There were no radios, TVs, or car radios in basic training and beyond.

1960s. Love and marriage. My first wife, Carolyn Klepfer Serle, and I had a television and a car with a working radio. That old Studebaker left a trail of oil and black smoke wherever it went. We watched the popular music shows and got out a little. Chubby Checkers comes to mind. Elvis was going strong, and when the Beatles conquered America. Rock and Roll was king.

We loved:

> *Yellow Submarine*
> *It's now or Never*
> *Stop in the Name of Love*
> *Heard it Through the Grapevine*
> *The Lion Sleeps Tonight*
> *These Boots Are Made for Walking*
> *Help Me Rhonda*
> *Dream, Dream, Dream*

Skip to now…Now – Let me just say, in no particular order, Willie, Bing, Dean, Sammy, Kris Kristofferson, Johnny Cash, Patsy Cline, Barbra Streisand, Lady Gaga, Celine Dion, Judy Garland, Vaughn Monroe, Julie Andrews, Mary Martin and Elvis. Show tunes, Rock and Roll, Country, Country Crossover and Frédéric Chopin.

Grazing through the names, knowing that I have overlooked monumental performers and performances that moved me, all I can say is, **"Alas. That is my nature."**

Frédéric Chopin

Elvis Presley

REPO MAN
WORKING AT THE FIRST NATIONAL BANK OF MIAMI.

I started on December 15, 1959, and my last day at the bank was August 18, 1967. After I graduated from the University of Miami in 1965, I was transferred to the Collections Department, as an outside man. Mostly I visited delinquent customers and collected payments, repossessed cars, and investigated "Skips." I had worked at the big bank for just over two years at this point.

After a time, I was promoted to be a desk man collecting delinquent accounts by phone. There was a hierarchy in our collections department. Outside man, Fifteen-day desk, Thirty-day desk, Unit Manager, Charge-off manager, Assistant Collections Manager Pete Bellows, Collections Manager James A. Faircloth.

John A. Faircloth was a bank officer whose rank was Assistant Cashier. He reported to Bob Lytle, Assistant Vice President who reported to the Vice President of Installment Loans, William Howard who reported to Senior V.P. John Sessions. The President and Chairman of the board was Harry Hood Bassett. The fact that I remember the names of these men, and the many other men and women that I worked with is due to the enormous influence they had on my happiness, education, and welfare over an eight-year employment period

The higher-ups weren't all tough, type-A, chain-smoking, alcoholic sons-of-bitches. There were a few good guys. By and large they were often mad at each other and at life and they concocted a strange and harsh regime. It was the devil I knew, so I stayed on, grateful to have a job. After a couple of years in Collections I was promoted to the Direct Lending Section where we received and processed Loan Applications from the "Walk-In' public.

A couple of stories you ask...? Well, OK. But remember, banking is such a dry business.

Here's a vignette from the direct Lending Department: I'd been with the bank for several years and I was taking loan applications and closing installment loans for people who came directly to the bank. There were about ten people in the Direct Lending Section.

IRATE CUSTOMER

We rotated the duty of calling rejected applicants before the close of business each day. I had the duty of calling rejected loan applicants one day when I encountered a particularly eloquent and disgruntled customer who needed a $400.00 loan to help with birthing expenses. Mrs. Krutz was about to deliver, and she didn't want to hear that we wouldn't be lending her the money.

"Excuse me," she said, "We really need the money. My husband's insurance doesn't cover obstetrics. You are our last hope. We always pay our bills, and our credit is excellent. You must make this loan!"

It was almost quitting time, and I was tired, but I had a personal need to make even rejected applicants feel good. "Look Mrs. Krutz. It's just that you are a little overextended according to the bank policy. You can get the money elsewhere. Your own bank won't turn you down."

"They already have," she sobbed. "I'm due today and we have to have money for the hospital. Please," she was begging, "You can help me. I know you can. Please!!!"

"So," I calmly responded, "Go to Beneficial Finance. They'll do it for you." I knew this from personal experience. Beneficial always came through.

"You Bastard," she hissed. "You people are all the same! Listen carefully..." She banged the phone down so hard it hurt my ear. I remember this conversation so well because I married the lady just a few years later. My how the world turns.

MY BOSS WAS DON STONEAKER

We called him Stoney. He bade me sit close to him. "Judith Anne Chan," he whispered hoarsely.

It was 8:30 a.m. on a fine Monday in June 1965. "Bill," he said, gazing into my eyes to make sure I was present. "We gotta get this car." It was a red 1961 Ford Galaxy Sunliner convertible – top of the line. Three payments past due. Owner's whereabouts unknown. It was time for Outside Man to go into action.

I went to Judith's last known address, an ordinary Southwest Miami tract home in a working-class neighborhood. No Luck. The house was empty and the clean garbage cans gave me zero clues.

I was Stoney's only hope.

Then a few days later we get a big break. A money order for a payment drifted in. It was purchased in Miami Beach. I took Don Dodson, a new man, with me to repo the car. I went to the drug store where the money order was bought but could not sweet talk them into giving me an address for Judith.

So, we went into bloodhound mode and scoured the neighborhood, looking for a red Ford Convertible. And then, to our surprise, we found it.

It was unlocked, rag top opened - in the driveway of a little apartment house. A sharp looking ride.

I found a mailbox box marked Chan but got no answer when I rang the bell. So, I did what came naturally. I prepared to repo the car.

First, we popped the trunk and emptied everything we found into a cardboard box carried for the purpose and stripped out the glove compartment contents. I would hot-wire the car when I was ready to start it. Steering wheel locks were not yet invented. Easy peasy.

"HEY! What do you think you're doing?" It was her landlord who had pulled a big black Buick in, behind the convertible, to block us from moving it. I realized that we should have just hot-wired the car and packed it up later.

"Repossession sir. First National Bank of Miami." That normally worked.

"No way. That's Judith's car and you ain't taking it until she says it's OK."

He told me her 'roommate' worked about a block away. I left Don to watch over the car and hot-footed it to the roomy's office – a travel agency. She didn't have a key but told me that Judith was waiting tables at a deli just a few blocks away. Again, leaving Don to watch the car, I drove to the deli and came face to face with Judith.

I sat at the counter and waited for her to come to me. She was a petite, pretty young thing. No sign of the horns or scales that I imagined her to have were in sight. She had a nice smile, a cute figure and was dressed in white. "Can I help you?"

"I'm here to repossess your car, Miss. I need you to give me the keys."

She gave me a horror-stricken look and moved away to take care of a customer. I waited. She returned and explained, "Hey. I just sent in a payment. Can you check your office, please? I'll have the rest very soon."

"No, sorry. I need the car now, but you can go down to the bank and fix things up with them yourself."

My heart was heavy, but I had to be firm. She left me again several times to do her work while I waited. She cried. She pled her case. I refused to listen.

Finally, she cracked and went to a purse hanging on the wall to fish out a set of keys. "You Bastard. Take the fucking keys!" She threw them at my face – hard. I ducked so I only got a little scratch on my left ear.

As I calmly exited through the front door I heard a customer signal her, "Oh Miss. There's something wrong with this chicken salad..."

Judith was having a bad day.

I gave the landlord her things and drove off with the top down, making Don Drive the bank's Ford Falcon.

Stoney was proud of me. "Good job Bill! Thank you."

Then the shit hit the fan. Judith sued the bank, its officers and me, for harassment, embarrassment, trespassing, and assault. I had to give a deposition at our lawyer's office a year or so later.

Joe Black, the lawyer, said, "Hey Bill. Good story." Typically, neither Stoney nor I ever got the back end of the story. The bank played everything close to the chest and the result of the case is unknown to me.

There were many repossessions, but I can only remember one other name by name – Slobber Lee Brown. He owed just one more payment and they made me take his car. He'd been consistently late with payments for 35 months and the bosses were paying him back for being a pain.

I assume he got his car back. I hopee!!! He was a likable guy. His sin was being black and having a nice car. I think my superiors at the bank were being racist.

DOING A FAVOR

We had a reciprocal agreement with a New England bank, wherein we would work their field collections and they would do ours. I was assigned to repossess a sporty mustang from a delinquent customer. Let's call him Fred.

I knocked on Fred's door and explained that I was there to repossess his car. He invited me in and was quite pleasant about the matter.

I'd already spoken to the Providence Rhode Island banker and volunteered to deliver the car to their door free of charge! I had orders to report to The U.S. Navy Construction Battalion (Sea Bees) Training School in Davisville, Rhode Island in a few days. My annual Coast Guard active duty for training. It would save me travel expenses and I'd enjoy a 36-hour road trip.

So, I told Fred that I'd deliver the car to the bank for him and save him $400.00 which the bank would add to his balance before selling the car.

"Great. Thank you very much. Only thing is, Bill, I'm tuning the motor, plugs and carburetor. The car's not drivable just now... I could put it together, but it will take two hours. It's late. Why don't you come back in the morning, and it'll be all ready to go?"

"Thanks Fred." It was after nine and I was more than ready to call it a day. "I'll see you at about ten in the morning." We shook hands.

Ten o'clock the next day – a sunny morning.

"Come in Bill. It's put back together. Come on into the garage and check out how well it will run."

Fred sat in the car and started it up. "See," he grinned up at me. "It's working perfectly." He gunned the motor and, to my alarm, kept it at high rpms for a while and, to my horror, the motor seized up.

Fred got out. Slammed the door. Handed me the keys. "Oops." His face was angry and resentful. "There was no oil in the engine. It will never run again."

So, I called a tow truck and found another way to go to my school in Rhode Island. It involved two uncomfortable days on a Greyhound bus.

GANGSTA REPO

Stoney called me at home. "Bill. John Ruggerio, the mobster, is three payments past due." His voice was hoarse as he filled me in. I could tell he was emotional.

"I just got a tip that he's staying at the old Miamian Motel on Brickell Avenue. I want you to go there and snatch the car before he wakes up in the morning." He gave me the particulars on the car – a big black Caddy.

Thus, it was. I met the tow truck at 4:30 a.m., a block away from the motel, and we reconnoitered the parking area. No Caddy. Persisting, on foot, I found it in back of the motel.

There was an open bathroom window with a light on and the shower was running. I could see the top of the gangster's head. I was scared. Stoney's raspy words rang in my head. "Don't let him catch you. He's got a violent reputation."

So, swift as a flash, I had the tow man drive around back and do a 'quick hitch.' But he made a lot of noise, and I could hear voices from the room as I got in my car and left the scene feeling like a superhero.

REPO REPO

There was a case involving a delinquent county employee with a Chevy Impala. Stoney sent me and Hank Lowery out to try to find and recover the vehicle. We spent a morning scouring downtown parking lots and found saw lots of Chevvies, but not the one we wanted.

Hot, and sick from sun exposure, we were about to give up. We found the car in the last lot we had decided to check.

We jimmied the lock and hot-wired the car. We drove it to the third floor of the bank's parking garage, near the installment loan department. Mission Accomplished! Stoney was proud and Hank and I felt like super sleuths.

I was called into the office the next day to show the car to the appraisal guy. No one could find it, and neither could I. Turned out that the customer had made a payment at a teller's window, gone into the garage, and re-repossessed it from us!

Being very busy with other cases, I lost track of what happened next, but I was proud of the client. He had shown initiative.

COLLECTIONS DEPARTMENT INSIDE MAN

I was in school at the University of Miami five nights a week and took a two-week service school every summer as a part of my Coast Guard Reserve duties. Plus, one weekend a month, I would put in two long days of training – the main requirement for being a reservist. I busy and stressed out all the time.

One bank promotion brought a big decrease in benefits. They moved me inside, so I lost the use of a company car. My assigned vehicle had been a VW Karman Ghia. It was sporty but had no A.C. No one else had cool air either, since factory-air had not yet become a thing.

For two-and-a-half years I had driven my company car home every night and never had to pay for gas, repairs, inspections, or anything. Personal use was permitted. Now I was scrambling to find a way to commute the nineteen miles from South Miami Heights to downtown Miami, go to school, go to Coast Guard Reserve meetings in North Miami, and visit my folks in Fort Lauderdale and Carolyn's in Miami. Worst promotion I ever had.

Arnold Wenzloff, a fellow collector, had a dandy little Volvo but no license to drive. I hooked up with him as we had the same hours and lived very close. When he vacationed, I bussed, drove myself, or hitched with others as opportunities arose. We, who worked for the bank, had to watch our pennies.

In the Collection Department a new hire would start as an outside man chasing delinquent customers and payments away from the bank. The next step would be working inside, calling customers who were fifteen days late on a payment. When sufficiently seasoned he would take a thirty-day chair.

Women were not used to do that kind of work then. They would be only hired for clerical or secretarial jobs. There was a saying, men need the better jobs because, 'they had families to feed.' How unfair this seems now.

I worked my way up through the chairs. Fifteen days. Thirty Days. Unit Manager. We had dial phones but no computers, no copy machines, cell phones, e-mail, electric calculators or adding machines. We used ball point pens and wrote everything that customers promised in shorthand. Our watchwords were, "Keep your fingers in the dial."

H pp nlt 19. S unempl. Sick. FU 20 (Translation = Husband promised to pay no later than the 19th. Spouse unemployed due to sickness. Follow up if no payment received by 20th.)

The notation system worked great. We began our collection efforts fifteen days after the due date. It made sense to outwait the ten-day late-fee kick in. We tried not to let accounts remain delinquent beyond our report dates, the day we'd have to hand accounts over to a higher-up who might be critical of slack efforts or softness.

DIGNIFIED BANKING, NOT

We were hard on our customers. Our system was stupid. The bank is no longer in existence.

When I was unit manager, Dave L., my fifteen-day man came to me with a problem. A customer refused to talk to him. The loan payment was $15.00, and their kids were screening the calls. I told him to pretend to be a friend. He learned that the customer was bowling. "With our loan repayment money," I reminded Dave. I told Dave to start calling bowling alleys until he found the customer. He did – customer got mad and hung up on him.

"So, Bill – what now?"

"Call him back," I advised, "and this time – you hang up on him." Dave did as I suggested and reported that he made sure to hang up hard!

"Now what Bill?"

I was in a bind. How to get past this without the customer coming to the bank and complaining about us? The only thing I could think of was to ask Dave to call him again and apologize.

He did and it seemed that the apology was well received. They made a date to meet at a bar the next night and have a friendly beer. Dave not only got the payment and a free beer, but he also made a friend, and there were no more problems until we had to let Dave go for getting arrested stealing hubcaps while using the bank's car, as an outside collector, a few months later.

PROMOTION

Then I was promoted to the direct lending department and later to Assistant Credit Analyst, working for Fred Tutt, Assistant Cashier, the Installment Loan Department's Credit Analyst. This was an interesting job.

I always called him Mister Tutt, as he was called when we first met at the American Institute of Banking class where he taught 'Analyzing Financial Statements.'

When he was promoted to Assistant V.P., Commercial Loan Department. I got Mr. Tutt's job, a little office, some more loan authority, and a secretary to take care of correspondence and type reports. We had a dandy dictating machine. But there was no raise in pay and no title – darn it!

My little section was responsible for reviewing all installment loans over $10,000. (That was a lot of money back then.) I analyzed the monthly profit and loss statements for our 'floor-planed' dealers. (Mostly Ford Car dealerships.) the technical name for this type of financing is Trust Receipt Financing.

My section was responsible for handling all loans over $10,000. This meant boats, airplanes, and business loans. I learned a lot, enjoyed working with both the numbers and the customers.

I had come to love the banking business but got lured away by a customer who promised a good job at a much higher salary.

It was a big surprise when the company that I had just turned down for a loan called me to ask if I would consider working for them. The money offered was much better and the job seemed interesting.

That will be a story for another day…

FAMILY TRADITIONS

I always loved my folks. And they loved me back although I suspect they liked my sister better. (Lol – I like her better too.)

Mom, née Edna Ketchum Conover, was born in 1905 and Dad, William Thomas Serle, Sr. in 1910. So they were young still when I came along in 1937 and younger when my sister Jan arrived in 1932. I'm sure Jan would tell this story differently and maybe better.

Family legend is that they met at Camp Karamac at the Delaware Water Gap. This was an inexpensive camp where young men and women could meet and play on vacation. They slept in rustic cabins or tents.

Activities would include swimming in the Delaware River, playing cards, badminton, boating, tennis, beauty and dance contests, and concerts. There must have been communal family-style meals, evening singing around campfires and maybe even a little romance? Nestled among the cabins was a large recreation hall known as the Wigwam. There was a dance floor, stage, and band.

For many years I thought that the camp was in Pennsylvania in the town of Delaware Water Gap. When my wife and I moved to New Jersey we discovered that the camp was on the New Jersey side of the Delaware River.

The Camp is gone now- just a woodsy spot with an historical marker where hikers park. I lived nearby and have visited the site several times alone, as well as with Daisy and with my great niece Meg Johnson and her boyfriend.

In addition to my existence and that of much the wonderful family around me that would not be possible without Mom and Dad, there is a trace of Karamack that reverberates in my heart and in my ears at family gatherings.

When the week at Camp Karamac was ended, some campers would depart, and newies would arrive. Good-byes at the Railroad station would often be tearful. So, they sang a song to ease the hurt, to the tune of the *Farmer In The Dell*:

> ***We hate to see you go,***
> ***We hate to see you go,***
> ***We hope to hell you never come back,***
> ***We hate to see you go.***

In my family, eight decades later, when we part after a visit, we still sing the song. Loud. If there are tears, they are a little easier to bear with the joke song in the air.

Edna caught Bill's eye. I picture her playing bridge with her girlfriends. She must have looked very sophisticated and alluring. Smoking cigarettes and telling jokes with Bill glued to her elbow, kibitzing.

A divorcee, Edna Conover was five years older than Bill. He lived with his mother Elizabeth

Hertle (nee Donahue) in Brooklyn. He worked at the Brooklyn, New York power station generating electricity for the subway system. Imagine that-a guy with a job during the depression! Mom was working as a secretary.

Edna was living with her sister's family, Belle Helmer, husband Bert and their infant daughters Joan and Dorothy.

This may not have been a comfortable arrangement for them as Mom smoked. Bert wouldn't tolerate tobacco use. Mom used to smoke in the bathroom with the window open. So out of the frying pan and into the fire of another marriage she went. But she loved Bill, and he loved her.

My paternal grandmother Nana, Mom, Dad, my sister Janice and I all lived together in Brooklyn, New York.

Jan and I are still kicking but the rest of our little tribe has passed on. Another tradition has sprung up, originating in 1985. It was a family photo taken in the stairwell of my sister's house in McLean, Virginia. On the all-to-rare occasions we gather there in number we try to get a snapshot.

I will share these few photos with you. The cast changes a little each time due to attendance, death and divorce.

Gleams in the eyes turn into babies. Babes become men and women. But we always sing the song upon departure.

Family gatherings with my sister Jan Newburg and her husband Art are treasured memories. Thanksgiving, weddings, special birthdays and other, motives triggered the gatherings

– not every year but often enough to become a family tradition. They were wonderful hosts.

The photos here do not, by any means, represent the entirety of the family. Geographical, financial and health issues were limiting factors.

The Newburgs had, a generous residence. Still, there were often people bunking on the floor in the rec room at these parties.

Judging by the age of the children, **this is a 1980ish photo**, notable because all six siblings are in it. I'm hidden behind Brother Larry Grinnell. • In the back row next to me stands Brother Guy Serle, my son Jeff, Son-in-Law Randy Perkins, Art Newburg, Dad William, Senior and Doug Newburg. ••Next row Brother Larry, Sister Nancy Riley, Daughter Kim Perkins, Sister Jan, Annie Newburg, ••• Then Christina Johnson, Billy's girlfriend DVM Cindi Levinson, the Fabulous Daisy Alonso Serle, Daughter Kris, Stepmom, Dorothea Serle, Raquel Grinnell, Marisa and Sandy (Norman) Grinnell. ••••Gary Johnson, baby Samantha, Billy Serle (William III), Michelle Grinnell.

This seems to be around 1998. Death and divorce have changed the cast, but new births and the growth of the children swells the ranks. All six sibs are here. Jan, me, Sandy, Larry, Nancy and Guy. New faces in the front row include sons In-Law Dan Keck and Ken Matthews. Guy's wife Tracy stands next to him. Guy, Chris Johnson and Kris Keck are responsible for the littlest kidneys.

143

2004ish. I am six-foot-four-inches tall, but my brother Guy and son Jeff make me look short. All of these children are grown-ups in 2022 as I publish this book. Some have children of their own.

2015ish (?) Serle, Newburg, Keck, Grinnell, Fish, Riley.
The old folk are fading and the new generations flourish.
So many missing for geographic and other reasons.
(Death, divorce, opportunity and geography.

SUMMERTIME

My Hometown ~ Like most Brooklynites, in the 1940's, we had electricity, private indoor plumbing, a telephone and sticky old windows that were hard to open. We also had an urgent need to get to the beach or the country on hot summer days. Unfortunately, for most of the adults, there were only stuffy offices, sweltering shops, and tedious subway commutes. Air conditioning was a dream.

Only movie houses had AC and advertised, '20 degrees cooler inside.' This was a powerful message because home television sets were still in the dreaming stage. We got our first television set when I was 13-years old.

Nevertheless, I adored summer as only a child with good friends, free time, energy and ample opportunities for adventure can love.

I was lucky to go to summer camps, for entire seasons, from my 9th thru my 12th years. So, I have a rich bag of summer memories. *City and Country.*

We moved to Farmingdale, Long Island when I was 14-years old. That too contributes to the variety of my recollections 85 youthful and adult years in New York, Florida, the mountains of western North Carolina, and rural northern New Jersey.

Defining Summer in Brooklyn ~
- Laying abed with open windows, listening to the Church Avenue trolley cars rumble.
- Going to Farragut Pool with my sister.
- Awaiting that special day when peach ice cream would finally make an appearance at the Bryers Ice Cream Store. In winter it was mostly chocolate and vanilla.
- Sitting on the front stoop watching fireflies and heat lightning.
- Jones Beach on special occasions to play in the Atlantic waves.
- Erasmus Hall High School – playing hooky.
- My first girlfriend.
- Nights when it was too hot to go to sleep comfortably.

At Camp Grant for Boys ~ Wildwood, New York
Unpaved tracks to the lake or the Long Island Sound where dust would rise comfortably through our toes with each barefoot step.
- Cicadas racketing in the evenings and loons wailing as the sun rose.
- Fireflies and heat lightning.
- Nights when it was too hot to go to sleep comfortably.
- Coastal adventures in the 20-man (boy) 'War Canoe.' Singing,

> *Our paddles keen and bright.*
>
> *Flashing like silver.*
>
> *Swift as the wild goose flight.*

Dip, dip and pull away...

Five Mile River Boy Scout Camp ~ Upstate New York

- Sleeping in a tent all summer
- Playing on the banks of the bracingly cold, clear Delaware River.

On Long Island, New York ~ Farmingdale

- Play in the Woods, and then pick off the ticks.
- The drive-in movie theaters.
- Mowing the damn grass.
- Having a girlfriend.
- Nights when it was too hot to go to sleep comfortably.
- Farmingdale High School.
- Hofstra College – on my own for a while.

In Fort Lauderdale ~ We moved to Florida when I was 18. Dad was seeking his fortune in the air conditioning business. This didn't work out so well in the long run. Mom was ill and died young. Dad had some hard times in business followed by a short visit to the Dade County Jail. I was an indigent student with two or three part-time jobs in addition to my winter class schedule.

- Nights when it was too hot to go to sleep comfortably.
- Having girlfriends.
- Working terrible outdoor jobs in the red-hot summer's school break. (I didn't realize how bad

they were then. In retrospect, I could have done better.)

Florida has now been my home, on and off, for over half a century.

The Miami days ~ School. The Coast Guard Reserve at the age of 19 – a 30-year, part-time career.

- Driving cars through the Miami heat before auto air conditioning was common.
- I was the outside man (with no AC in the car) at the First National Bank of Miami's Installment Loan Department for several years. I stayed with the bank for eight years. It was my first adult job. I got married. Had children. Graduated from the University of Miami, after a decade of classes, mostly at night, whilst working as a banker.
- Drive-in movie theaters.
- Mowing the damn grass.
- Nights when it was too hot to go to sleep comfortably.

There were many joyful elements too. My growing family, the pleasures of swimming in the surf or at a community pool and much more. I learned the joy of sailing on Biscayne Bay. And, finally, window air conditioners became commonplace.

Cape May, New Jersey ~ Coast Guard Boot camp was a six-month hiatus. Learning how to be a Coast Guardsman is not an easy task, but I enjoyed it as a respite from being a destitute student at the University of Miami.

Meals, housing, transportation and education were free, and I received a $35.00 monthly salary and free food! I spent an interesting month aboard the Coast Guard Cutter Unimak and a month in Groton, Connecticut to round out my six-month active-duty commitment. Then back to my then-current hometown – Miami.

Bryson City and Waynesville, North Carolina ~ We moved to the mountains of North Carolina and didn't need air conditioning for over 20 wonderful years. White-water canoeing, hiking the mountain trails, and more.

Allamuchy, New Jersey ~ At long last, a certain prosperity was achieved in our retirement years. Off to New Jersey, for our twilight years, we thought. I built and sailed a little skiff on the local lakes and enjoyed hiking and biking the rural byways and trails.

Then things changed and we moved first to Rockledge, Florida and then to Flagler Beach.

Rockledge Florida ~ Back in sunny Florida for some 15 blessed years now. I'm a happy, airconditioned, citizen. Here, the seasons are reversed. At some time in October the windows were opened to admit balmy breezes and give my electric bill took a break.

I liked sitting in our home office-library to watch the little model sailboat on the windowsill dance in the breeze. It heels and I pretend that it is at sea on a fine summer day – me at the helm!

My beautiful, real, handmade, sailboat lived on a trailer in my garage and was not used often enough. It now lives in a grandson's garage and is still not used often enough.

Flagler Beach Florida ~ I pass happy days writing in my office and helping clients publish. I pass happy days playing poker on Fridays, and several times a month, go hobnobbing with fellow writers in both Ormond Beach and Rockledge.

I gifted my boat to Grandson Brandon Serle who maintains it and its trailer in 'Bristol' fashion.

Cousins, Captain Brandon Serle and First Mate Melissa Serle, enjoy a Halifax River cruise aboard *Day's Ease.*

Setting sail on the Rockledge windowsill.

THE WORKER

I take pleasure in work. It's fun, don'tcha know. No matter if it is a literary project, a chore, or just building a shelf for my wife.

Daisy and I remodeled our Chippendale style cabinet in May of 2020. We acquired the elegant piece in North Carolina fifteen years ago on the very day that we moved to New Jersey. We admired its ornate style and stately presence. We stopped at the Asheville furniture store and added it to the back of the rental truck to keep company with the boxes and mishmash of our belongings. We had no furniture then because we'd sold our mountain home furnished.

The cabinet became a large television stand in our new home.

Three years later it moved, again, when we relocated to Rockledge, Florida and it became foyer furniture for eight wonderful years. I drilled a few holes in the back and installed halogen lights to illuminate the interior.

It moved to Flagler Beach, Florida in 2017 and reverted to its TV stand role. And it was fine until we declared that we wanted our home decorations to be 'beachy.' It no longer fit in.

"Let's paint it white!" enthused Daisy.

I agreed after a long discussion of the many reasons it might be *too much* work. Once the paint was purchased and the job started, it became fun.

All doors, hinges, knobs, latches, mullions and lots of miscellaneous hardware were removed. The four glass panes were taken out and measured. We ordered four mirrors to replace the glass.

We draped our nine-foot-long kitchen island in contractor's paper and used it as a workstation for painting the doors with several coats of bright white.

Painting the cabinet itself turned out to be a joy. It looked wonderful to our eyes. After several coats of the brilliant white, Nick, our strong and

2011
It looked something like this before we
remodeled it.

2020

handsome grandson, helped us move it to the deck bench where we laid it on its back to remove the legs and replace them with the invisible, I hoped, solid wood, black base that I'd made. The cabinet should now seem to float above the floor. Shopping and painting had consumed a week, with multiple trips to Lowes and the mirror company.

Now everything went in reverse. Move the cabinet back inside and reinstall shelves, hardware, mullions, mirrors, doors and knobs, restock the shelves with china and platters, etc. Rewire the lights to shine back to the wall to give it a halo of light. The entire project took about a week.

Later, in further celebration of our television-watching hobby, we bought swivel recliner chairs, a couch, a coffee table, a side table, and a smart 55-inch Samsung television to complete our room.

We replaced the new tabletops with rustic, beachy, cedar planks and made a lamp base with the chunky leftover wood.

Old Chippendale now looks even more elegant to my eye – especially when the late afternoon sun lights it up. The halo-effect works. The mirrors won't reveal clutter should our occasional messiness strike. They just reflect the room.

I am ready for the next project.

2022

SAFE PLACES

The topic of safe places came to mind last night when visiting with my nephew Doug and my sweet wife Daisy on the phone. T'was a three-way conversation.

Doug is my sister Jan's caregiver. His mom has dementia, the after-effects of covid, and the deteriorating effects of a marvelous 89-year life. He, overcome by the health problems that his own 62 years of age have brought, is stressed by his life situation – twenty-four/seven duties. He gets minimum help from family members due to geography and such, to the point where he sought support from a psychologist.

He said, "I was doing a session with Karen, my psychologist, that involved breathing exercises, closing my eyes, and imagining a safe place. It helped center me and improve my mental state. My safe place was sitting on the beach in Nags Head in North Carolina's Outer Banks. At night. All alone. No stress."

Daisy chimed in, "The beach! Me too!

"Doug. I've had a lot of depression, and my shrink taught me to go to my safe place – by the sea."

Our three-way conversation led me to think about my safe place.

I decided that my safe place was in the tiny cabin of a certain sailboat. The 'PocketShip.' The little John Harris-designed boat is only 14′ 10″ long and is easily trailered behind a small car to any waterway you might fancy. Halifax River in northeast Florida? Finger Lakes District in New York? The Florida Keys?

As cozy as it is, there is room enough for my six-foot-four-inch frame to stretch out, with my legs reaching into the space beneath the cockpit seats. And my brother Sandy (Norman Grinnell to some) could stretch out on the other side.

The mast and rigging can be set up at the boat ramp in fewer minutes than you might imagine. This sweet little craft sails faster than some bigger boats. It turns in its own length, and swing keel up, it draws just 16.″

In my 'Safe Place' reverie, I own a PocketShip. I'm at anchor in quiet water, with plenty of food and supplies for a week-long voyage from Biscayne Bay to Key Largo, Florida. I sit in the cabin. The silence is punctuated by occasional ripples brushing against the hull. The day's high adventure now a part of my history. Belly full. Love

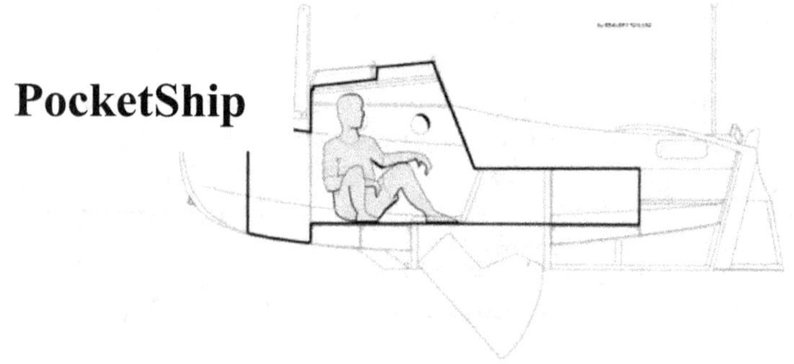

PocketShip

and the further pursuit of happiness await at my journey's end. Sigh. In my dreams…

I built a little sailing skiff, also designed by John Harris. I bought the 'JimmySkiff' kit from his company for about $3,000. It took me many happy hours to finish the project over a two-year period when I first retired to Northern New Jersey in 2005. I loved sailing my pretty little boat in the local lakes in New Jersey and, later, in the Indian River and Sykes Creek near our Rockledge, Florida home.

I first saw the prototype PocketShip when I visited the builder's facility in Annapolis, Maryland, in 2006. It was indoors, on a trailer, and ever so pretty. I'd made the day trip there to buy some brass hardware for my boat, accompanied by Daisy, sister Jan, and her husband, Art. While they were milling around looking at assorted nautical gear, I was invited to climb a ladder and have a closer look at the boat. I scrambled aboard and soon found myself sitting in the cabin, imagining that I had bought the plans and built my own PocketShip.

Leaning back, knees drawn up, I closed my eyes and had a moment of phantastic peace descend upon my soul. I was in my safe place, and it took an effort by my companions to bring me back.

I had a further moment aboard the PocketShip at the Annapolis Boat Show the following year. My brother Sandy, who lived in Annapolis, attended the show with me. We jumped at the opportunity to go for an hour's sail with designer John Harris and his girlfriend, Gloria.

The wind was too quiet, but the boat moved well enough anyway. There was plenty of room for the four of us, and we had a good visit.

Yes, I wanted to buy the kit. Life overran my half-baked plan, and now I have aged out. But, in my mind, the *safe place*, and the happiness it brings, remain firmly in my heart and mind.

My JimmySkiff is now in the capable hands of a favored grandson. Small boat magazines lead me to dream 'boating' from time to time. I sometimes slip quietly into a certain cabin.

Enjoy the photos and drawings.

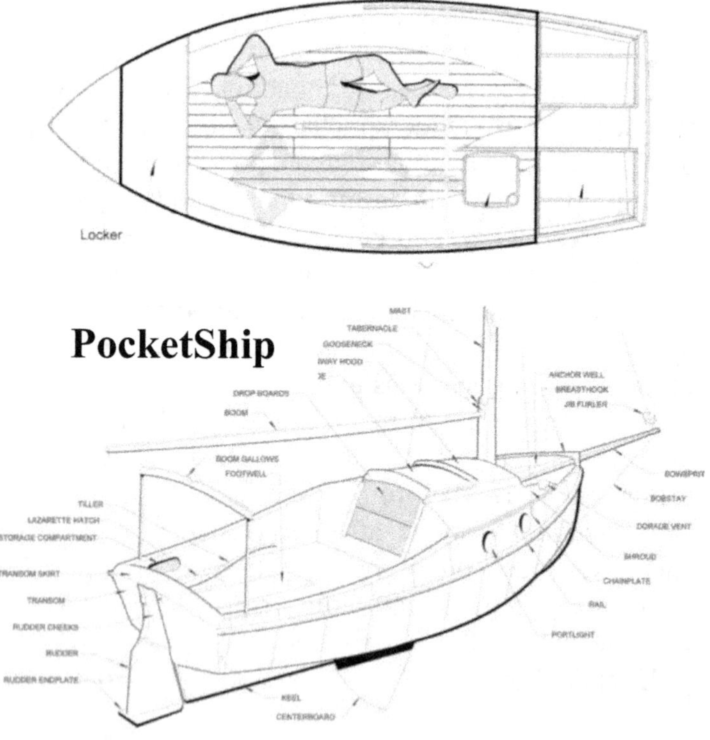

Safe place

A picture is worth a thousand words.

Above – Brother Sandy Grinnell, PocketShip designer John Harris, and Dreamer Bill at the helm.

Below – John dousing the mainsail. The jib is roller furled.

BONUS TIME

I remember my first bonus. T'was early January 1960. I'd been working at the First National Bank of Miami for just a month when Mr. Lytle called me to his office and handed me a check for $15.00.

"What's this," I stammered. Fearing that he was going to fire me.

He smiled and said, "It's your bonus for the two weeks you worked last year." I was so happy. I could have kissed his alligator shoes.

I was earning $60.00 a week and just getting by. That bonus would be worth more than $150.00 in today's (2022) money.

Bonuses can be fantastic.

What I mean to write about, however, is bonus time. Life span. Life expectancy.

The estimated maximum human life span is about 125 years. Our bodies wear out. Compare that to some trees that may live for over 7,000 years.

The average human life span, birth through death, has been going up over the millenniums. Early hunters might have averaged 20 years. Middle Ages life spans were about 45 years, and today Americans average 78 years. I'm 84, and so might claim that I've had a bonus of six years.

There is more nuance to this subject. For instance, if one twin dies at birth and the other lives 80 years, the average for that small group is a 40-year life span. That does not describe anything useful. Remember, 94.3% of statistics are just made up – as I made up most of these numbers.

Infant mortality, war, murder, accidents, disease, and infection skew the numbers. Some exceptional people have always lived longer lives over the ages.

Jesus died at the age of 33. MLK at 37. RFK 43. JFK 46. Alexander Hamilton 49. My mother 52. Abe Lincoln 54. FDR 63. Imagine how our world might have changed if these minds and spirits had been graced with long bonus years. Peace, love, forgiveness, happiness, and prosperity might have been more universal.

As the average life span increased, grandparents became more available to share knowledge and culture, thus improving life for all.

In today's world, writing, the internet, media, and modern communications help us share culture and knowledge. Grandparents are a bonus.

Think about how the average person from the year 1000 A.D. would view today's modern machines and conveniences. His mouth would drop open at the use of flush toilets and running water in the electrically lit house with a Ring doorbell.

If you could sleep and wake up in the year 3000 A.D., you'd probably experience shock and awe. Magic. Anti-gravity vehicles that need no steering wheels, no roads, no traffic signals, or highway police. 500-plus-years life spans cut short only by tired-of-living volunteers. Interplanetary colonization. Interstellar experimentation. Food production involving no cruelty to animals. Workers are so super-efficient that very few people are needed to do the essential jobs. Walking and talking walls. The two-hour work week. No brick-and-mortar banks, libraries, or post offices. Climate control – it will only rain on demand.

I've spent every bonus day doing things I enjoy and hoping that my life has been a blessing to those around me. What a marvelous dividend.

AMERICAN ESSAYS

A DREAM

Human beings flee from horrific situations. This has been going on since before the dawn of history. War, governmental persecution, unbearable crime, starvation, climate change, and other reasons cause people to leave.

They leave their work, homes, families, possessions, friends, familiar surroundings, native languages, churches, medical care, typical foods, everyday sanitary habits, comfort, customs and culture, pets, farm animals, savings, and, importantly, hope for a future in their own land.

Rarely are they met at borders with open arms, offers of assistance, food, shelter, blankets, and clean water.

There are some exceptions. Two come to mind: the American reception of Cubans in the 1960s and 70s, which I witnessed closeup, and the current international acceptance of Ukrainian refugees.

If you happen to be black, *fuhgeddaboudit*. You will likely die in misery rather than be welcomed to any new country. Especially in Europe where some three-thousand African refugees drowned in the Mediterranean last year.

I dream that people at our southern border will be met with compassion and treated according to U.S. laws. They are entitled to ask for asylum, to be given a court hearing with the counsel of an attorney and be free to remain in the United States while awaiting their court dates.

U.S.C. Title 8, Chapter 12 states: (1) In general, any alien who is physically present in the United States or who arrives in the United States (whether or not at a designated port of arrival and including an alien who is brought to the United States after having been interdicted in international or United States waters), irrespective of such alien's status, may apply for asylum in accordance with this section or, where applicable, section 1225(b) of this title.

Here's a question. Is it cheaper use military force to keep refugees out and imprison people who cross the border – or greet them with compassion and a bus ticket?

If we granted them the right to work while awaiting their day in court, it would benefit the economy in several ways. We need the workers and the taxes they will pay. And the refugee would be less vulnerable to abusive. employers.

And there is a big bonus. The children of these refugees, in the years to come, will be our respected and educated political leaders, philosophers, statesmen, physicians, and engineers to help solve the challenging problems that the future will bring. My dream.

I, for one, demand the separation of church and state. Yet, in accord with the principles of the people of the book, I would vastly prefer the practices of the Good Samaritan.

The Bible contains stories of immigrants and outsiders. Genesis narrates the journey of Abraham from his homeland to Canaan, a land occupied by other people, and tells how he and his family make their way in a territory and society where they have neither land nor kin.

Exodus, Leviticus, and Deuteronomy dictate, *"When a stranger resides with you in your land, you shall not wrong him. The stranger who resides with you shall be to you as one of your citizens; love him as yourself, for you were strangers in the land of Egypt"* *(Leviticus. 19:33-34).*

The book of Ruth is the story of a foreigner who comes to Israel, working as a laborer in the fields, hoping for a better life. The immigrant, Ruth, was an ancestor of King David and, through him, Jesus.

I have a dream.

WALLS

FEBRUARY 2022

ASSOCIATED PRESS
(Paraphrasing) – U.S. population growth has dipped to its lowest rate since the nation's founding. The U.S. grew by 0.1%, from July 2020 to July 2021. We have been experiencing slow population growth for years. This past year was the first time since 1937 that the nation's population grew by fewer than one-million people. Population growth has been slowing because of lower birth rates and decreasing net migration, while mortality rates rise due to the aging of our population.

~ ~ ~

As a mid-stream Democratic Conservative, I've long thought that walls between countries are bad ideas. The failure of the great Wall of China is but one *long* example. Two-thousand-four-hundred-miles in length and two-thousand-five-hundred-years old, it was formidable, but did not work. Determined people go around, over and under walls.

The Walls of Jericho, the *Maginot* Line, the Iron Curtain, the Berlin Wall, and the wall around my son's garden are but a few examples of failed walls.

The garden wall was intended to keep Harvey, the pet dog, from wandering the neighborhood. Sometimes he goes over or under but, more commonly, someone fails to close the gate, and Harvey's in the wind again.

I would propose a better 'Hands Across the Border' policy for Mexico, Canada, and the Caribbean Islands. It would consist of exchanging cultural programs and commercial opportunities and easy passage over the borders. It would be good for everyone. Perhaps even, one day, A union of all American countries like the European Union.

Ex-president Trump's idea of making the Mexicans pay for a wall was bad. The idea was ill-considered, insulting, and impractical. It seems to me that if we build a few bridges to ease the refugees' way into the States, the Mexican brain-drain could soon lead the foolish among them, *Donaldo Trumpoestos,* to propose a wall to keep people in!

When I was in the Christmas Tree business, I had a tree lot in a large Texas border town. Many of my customers seemed to be 'Mexican.'

I liked to chat my customers up at the cash register, and I heard this story several times, usually in a soft, slightly accented voice.

I'd ask, Brooklyn accent, "Where ya from?"

The reply was usually, "San Antonio."

"How long have yuh lived here?"

"All my life. My family has been here for over five-hundred years."

My good experiences in that 'border town,' led me to rethink about what it might mean to be an 'American.' Those Mexicans were, in fact, way more American than me and much more Texan than yours truly was North Carolinian. And they bought my quality Fraser Fir Christmas trees.

There is the morality of immigration policy to be considered. We are mostly 'People of the Book;', Jews, Muslims, and Christians. Our books tell us to be forgiving,* charitable,** and, importantly, to 'Love our neighbors as we love ourselves.'***

I strongly believe in secular government, but I am undeniably influenced by the moral fabric of my countrymen.

Some of the benefits from adopting my 'Hands Across the Border' policy might be:

- Finding labor to work in our current unfilled-jobs economy.
- Adding to our Social Security and tax bases.
- Freeing certain federal thugs**** to be retrained to do more meaningful work such as collecting taxes from billionaires, helping the homeless, and such.
- Enhanced cultural diversity.
- Eased international relations.
- Heeding humanitarian concerns.
- Creating more customers who could afford to buy 'American' goods.
- Improving earnings for Trailways and Greyhound Bus Companies.

- Reducing our prison inmate population
- Sourcing inexpensive autos, maple syrup, coconuts, and *sombreros*.

Don't get me wrong. I would institute some strict controls at ports, borders and in airports. I'd insist that, when challenged, 'crossees' would need to test at least half human. I, after all, am a conservative.

* The Holy Bible
** The Holy Quran
*** Matthew 22
****Border Patrol Agents and ICE Agents.

GOOD NEWS

I grow weary of negative headlines and newscasters decrying the end of a 'kind and gentle' America. They say, "America is falling apart at the seams."

"Is Civil War inevitable?"

And even scarier, perhaps, "inflation. Inflation! INFLATION."

OMG. The sky is falling… not. Not! NOT.

Fear sells more newspapers and attracts more viewers because we are hardwired to survive a harsh world. We no longer need to fear tigers or flee fires that burst out without warning. We know in advance that tornadoes are near or that storms are brewing a thousand miles away.

I find America to be not only beautiful, but peopled with hard-working, caring citizens busy with a huge variety of occupations. Recent travels involved crossing Florida, Georgia South Carolina, North Carolina, Virginia, and Maryland borders. We did not have to stop at any of these state lines to show 'papers.' There are signs of good governance everywhere.

Daisy and I were taking a trip to visit relatives in South Carolina and Virginia. There were billboards saying, 'Welcome to Georgia,' or 'We're glad you came to North Carolina,' etc. Not only were there no checkpoints at borders, but there are welcome centers where travelers could rest, use bathroom facilities, obtain maps and information, snacks, and cold beverages. Sometimes these snacks and beverages were offered without charge.

We can get cash from machines but really don't even need cash unless a poker game is in the offing. What a country!

I got out of my car to see if a South Carolina Waffle House was open. "Sorry. We're closed." Weary, I stumbled and fell in the dark parking lot. I struggled to get up. Daisy stood by, wringing her hands, paralyzed with fear for my safety.

As I rolled over to my stomach a truck driver ran up and helped me to my feet. A good Samaritan indeed. "Thank you." was all I needed to say. No thoughts of what section of the country we hailed from. No notice of the fact that I was a 'white' man, and he was 'black.' Just a good man helping someone in need. Thankfully, I was not injured.

Another sign of good governance is the state of the roads. There may have been an occasional bump or baby pothole but, by and large, the roads were smooth, well paved, quiet, beautifully maintained, and landscaped. It was like driving in a park. What a country!

I believe that if you pick two states at random, say Oregon and Mississippi or paired up Montana with Arizona, the people could speak to each other and understand our common language without any difficulty at all. What a country!

Our common language and the free flow of interstate commerce and travel makes it easy for businesses to obtain supplies and to recruit employees. It's simple enough to move your family two-thousand miles to pursue a better job or even happiness. No government permission needed. Just go for it.

Telephone calls, worldwide, are made without curly wires, or even picking up an instrument and 'dialing.' Easy and universal fuel availability, telephone communications, hotel, bathroom, and restaurant accommodations all ready when you are thanks to our good system of government. Sometimes the government's most important role is stay out of the way – refrain from making rules and regulations.

Finally, our system of taxation has created the world's greatest fund of treasure. I think we are moving toward taking care of all our people. What a country!

I believe that it's up to us, *the great unwashed public*, to be critical when hearing, reading, or watching 'The News,' and question whether it's journalism, editorial, opinion or show business. Good news is often unmentioned even though it more than offsets the bad.

We're not perfect but boy do we rock!

What a country!

WONDERFUL LAND OF OPPORTUNITY
1800 – A MESSY ELECTION

Many of us are stressed out this November 2020, as the election process proceeded at an irregular pace. We are used to seeing a sitting loser graciously concede and invite the winner to tea at the white house. My advice to my excitable wife, Daisy, was, "Relax. All will end well enough no matter the man in the white house. Our laws and institutions have enormous strength to resist the base intentions a few scoundrels on top."

Thank the heavens for our wonderful form of government and the genius of the great minds behind its creation.

The election of 1800 was also a mess. The Unites States of America was only 24 years old. Here's a little history lesson gleaned from Wikipedia and my reading of Ron Chernow's great biography, *Alexander Hamilton.*

The sitting President in 1800 was John Adams. He lost the election. There was a runoff between Thomas Jefferson and Aaron Burr.

The Federalists' man, Aaron Burr, favored a strong central government and close relations with

Great Britain. The Democratic-Republicans' man, Thomas Jefferson, favored decentralization to the state governments.

According to historian John Ferling, the jockeying for electoral votes, regional divisions, and propaganda smear campaigns made the election recognizably modern.

The constitution, at the time, did not allow for electors to choose a vice president but stipulated that the second-highest vote-getter would hold that office.

Instead of choosing Jefferson president and Burr vice president, the electors botched their work and instead awarded each man 73 electoral votes. The responsibility of breaking the tie was handed to the House of Representatives.

Each delegation from the 16 states was given one vote to award to either Jefferson or Burr. The winner needed to get nine of the 16 votes to be elected president, and the balloting started on February 6, 1801. It took 36 rounds of balloting for Jefferson to win the presidency.

Still dominated by Federalists, the sitting Congress loathed to vote for Jefferson – a partisan nemesis. Jefferson and Burr essentially ran against each other in the House. Votes were tallied thirty-five times, yet neither man captured the necessary majority of nine states.

Eventually, Federalist James A. Bayard of Delaware, under intense pressure and fearing for the future of the Union, made known his intention to break the impasse. As Delaware's lone representative, Bayard controlled the state's entire vote. On the thirty-sixth ballot, Bayard and three other Federalists cast blank ballots, breaking the deadlock, and giving Jefferson the support of enough states to win the presidency.

History teaches us that even flawed men can hold high positions.

Thomas Jefferson was a brilliant man and contributed much to our country, and to our ideas about freedom. He owned over 600 slaves. Jefferson wrote, ...We hold these truths to be self-evident, that all men are created equal...

Aaron Burr was a hot-headed lawyer-politician despised by Alexander Hamilton, the great architect of American government. As Vice President, Burr's most notable act was killing Hamilton in a duel. As a result of that crime, he lost everything, never recovered, and died broke, in obscurity in 1836.

Yes. The country has survived awful events. I believe we are still one wonderful land of opportunity.

A SAFE AMERICA

The United States of 1791 was far different from today's America. Few people had jobs as we know them today. People worked for themselves with some exceptions. Think Slaves and Merchant Seamen. Mercantile clerks and blacksmith apprentices were likely to be sons. Women rarely worked outside of their homes. Banks were small and one room schools were iffy.

There were no gas stations, movie theatres, telephone operators, call centers, railroads, insurance agencies, small-town libraries, police and fire departments, casinos, truck drivers, electricians, plumbers, steel mills, auto manufacturers or cabbies and, in general, few opportunities for folks to earn wages.

The thirteen states were each trying to govern independently. Folks didn't yet know what to make of the federal government. They didn't know if they could trust it to not become a monarchy. Most people were farmers and rural. Their tools were axes, spades, plows and long guns. The rifle hadn't been invented.

So, in 1791, as the Bill of Rights, as the first ten amendments to the U.S constitution were known, stated that, 'A well-regulated Militia, being necessary to the security of a free State, the right of the people to keep and bear arms, shall not be infringed.' The army and navy then were virtually non-existent. Today, the U.S.is arguably the most secure country in history with a well-regulated Army, Navy, Marine Corps, Space Command, Air Force and Coast Guard. Our reach is worldwide.

People today no longer need guns as tools with rare exceptions for self-protection. Guns are too common and cause many tragic deaths here when we compare our statistics to other developed nations. Also, guns are far more lethal today than were the old-fashioned muzzle loaders. A lone gunman can kill crowds of people with rapid fire weapons developed for warfare. Many things have changed but the words of the Second Amendment still cause fierce debate in this country, with attitudes shaped by the NRA and the congressmen under its spell.

So much has changed. It is time for us to begin to make effective regulations about weapons – one does not need a sub-machine gun to hunt deer. One needs a license to drive a semi or even a motorcycle. That which is dangerous to our national health should be licensed and regulated.

People with prison records should get permits before they're allowed to buy a gun. Same goes for minors and mentally disturbed people. Weapons of war should be regulated to permit them only for recreational purposes. Let's become a safer and more secure country.

A LOOK AT THE PRESIDENCY

I was thinking things over this morning and realized that there was a great diversity in our choice for president of the United States during my lifetime. Part of that variety had to do with where our presidents were born and raised, I made the following list:

STATE	PRESIDENT
New York	Roosevelt
Missouri	Truman
Kansas	Eisenhour
Massachusetts	Kennedy
Texas	Johnson
California	Nixon
Michigan	Ford
Georgia	Carter
Illinois	Reagan
Texas	Bush Sr.
Arkansas	Clinton
Texas	Bush
Hawaii	Obama
New York	Trump
Delaware	Biden

They had much in common. (Even though they had widely different backgrounds, families, wealth, education, and views on how to use the office.

For example:

- Each had both vehement detractors as well as ardent supporters.
- They each had their own understanding of government and the role of the office they held.
- All strove to improve American life but marched to the beat of different drums.
- They were all subservient to the will of the American people as exerted by separate but equal branches of government.
- Not least, they were held accountable by the 'Fourth Estate,' our free and independent press.
- Importantly, they were also subject to the rule of law as upheld by staunch government staffers and the lower courts.

It's a little hard for me to answer the question, "Who's your favorite president?" I liked each one of them at times but I aged to became a little more critical in my thinking.

My family and I have benefited muchly from programs of government beneficence such as Social

Security and Medicare. Roosevelt and Johnson lead the field here.

President Truman called for a National Health Insurance Program. It was created in 1965 when LBJ signed the Social Security Act. Johnson enrolled Truman as the first Medicare beneficiary and gave him with the first Medicare card – Truman's wife Bess got the second – at the signing ceremony,

We loved Kennedy for his charm and grace and lucky marriage. I was proud to have Obama as president because his election revealed something good about our national character.

Truman had a humble background and never attained the wealth of other presidents – somehow, I liked him because of this and his willingness to "let the buck stop here."

People can say something good about each of them… even President Trump. He is a wonderful dancer.

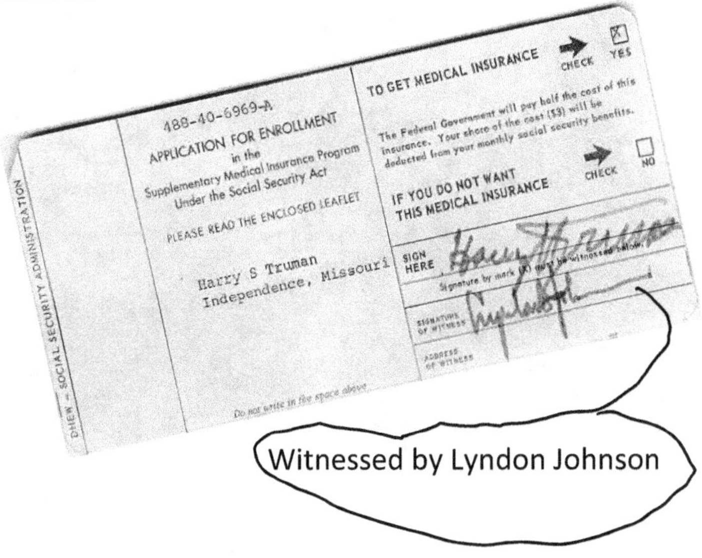

Witnessed by Lyndon Johnson

THE FIFTH ESTATE

A definition could center around the ability of its people to pursue happiness without interference from government – city, county, state or federal. And without fear of governmental violence against any member of our community.

I see signs of good governance every day. Sometimes the absence of problems is the result of good government – this is often invisible and rarely considered.

Locally, the garbage, recyclables, and lawn litter are picked up on a regular basis. It's easy to travel around town because citizens reliably follow the rules of the road. Emergency response time for medical, fire and accident incidents is very good. The libraries, parks and recreation centers are beautiful and accessible. Public transportation and food for the needy and shut-ins is easily available. Businesses of every stripe flourish. It is easy to vote. Education is free through secondary school and low-cost higher education is available. Street and other signs make it easy to get around.

State services including education, law enforcement, voting management, bridges, roads and licensing, unemployment insurance and child welfare, are firmly in place without being unduly burdensome. Clean air, parks and recreation, the licensing of drivers and craftsmen and much more are affected by state the governance.

The federal government takes care of Medicare and Social Security. They insure safe air travel, a reliable interstate highway system, national defense, consumer protection and much more.

PERSONAL FREEDOM

I can jump in my car or take a train for a journey of ten thousand miles with just the clothes I happen to have on. I just make sure that my phone and my wallet are in their habitual pockets and that I kiss my wife goodbye – not that I would ever dream of leaving her behind.

Let's say that the plan is to visit all fifty states. We will understand the rules of the road everywhere, enjoy meeting strangers, sleep safely in hotels, and find charging stations or fuel for my vehicle. We will be confident that restaurants and other merchants follow good sanitation practices. We'll be able to keep current on financial obligations and to manage our finances virtually anywhere. Citizens are mostly disposed to be hospitable and help one another if a need arises. *What a country!*

Now I know we are not perfect and that we must continually adapt to changing times. Our constitution and laws must be managed.

THE BIG PICTURE

I took an oath to defend the Constitution of the United States of America against all enemies, both foreign and domestic when I was sworn in as an officer in the United States Coast Guard some fifty-odd years ago. Most federal government officials, judges and members of congress take a similar oath – that means millions of government officials as well as military officers are obliged to do the right thing even if circumstances make it difficult.

CONSIDER:

- The military is subject to civilian oversight.
- The law of *posse comitatus* keeps the government from using the military to enforce laws over the civilian population.
- The three branches of government are co-equal and independent of each other.
- Government officials are servants of the people and not the other way around.
- Military officers and career government officials, as opposed to some political appointees, will resist, or refuse illegal orders.

In addition to the above, a free and independent press keeps watch for government misdeeds and missteps. They are called the Fourth Estate. The first three are the legislative, executive, and judicial branches.

I see the career government employees and military officers as THE FIFTH ESTATE.

The five estates offset and exert a steadying hand on each other.

America is a big, chaotic mess, and at the same time, still, ... "A beacon of hope to the world."

AMERICA, WHAT A COUNTRY!

I love the New York Times. I read it on my iPhone every morning. I get local news from the Daytona News Journal but rely on the New York Times and its 1,500 reporters to provide me with national and international news, business news and the cultural affairs of the world.

Just now, I read an interview with Michael Dell, founder and CEO of Dell computers. I had no prior information about his personal story, but the article gave me an introduction to Mr. Dell's life story and huge business success. It made me think about what makes America great and what we must continue to do and protect in order to maintain its greatness.

Michael Dell was born in 1965 to a middle-class family. His dad was an orthodontist and his mom a financial analyst. He grew up experiencing wonderful conversations around the dinner table exploring the politics of the day, finances, science and math. In school he excelled at math. He was geeky rather than athletic. He hung out at RadioShack rather than the local soda shop.

At 16, he bought an IBM PC with earnings from youthful entrepreneurial activities and investments. The money came from trading baseball cards and the buying and of selling silver and gold.

To his parents' astonishment he took the PC apart.

He figured out exactly what the different little sub-assemblies did and came to understand the nature of computers. PC's did not have hard disks at that time. As you may remember, we used floppy disks to store information back then.

Young Michael became adept at repairing and upgrading computers; understanding all that there was to know about them. He figured out that computers were assembled from parts that were

Michael Dell

commercially available. If one were to purchase the parts to make a computer, the cost would be about one-tenth of the retail price that consumers paid. He said he thought of Robber Barons when he realized how much money was being made in the industry.

Later he bought an Apple II Computer and promptly disassembled it to study the bits and learned how they work together to perform various functions.

As a freshman college student, he made a business out of upgrading computers for his college classmates. He said, "I got mixed up in a little side business of installing hard drives in computers to make them way more convenient to use."

His parents, of course, expected him to succeed as a student. When they learned of his business they objected and required him to abandon his business efforts and concentrate on his studies. An obedient son, he did stop his side business for a total of ten days. He then decided that his passion was the computer business. He went to work full-time and quit college – never to graduate.

In the interview, he went on to say that he rented a little office for the work. He outgrew his rental space in just thirty days and began a business that experienced phenomenal growth over many years. As you may know he is now a billionaire. He has donated over 2.5 billion dollars to fund his charitable foundation, and he is well respected in every corner.

In the article he was asked this question, "What about tech gets you excited today?"

"… while the last 35 years have been amazing, I think it's going to pale in comparison to what's coming." He went on to discuss 5G,* AI,** The IoT,*** and more.

Dell's words hit me up alongside the head. "We have, in this country, an engine that is creating a lot of new businesses, and a lot of new innovations that are globally relevant." He said, that "...as we progress through the years, we must always ensure that this ability – the ability to start new companies by entrepreneurs should be protected."

* 5G stands for Fifth Generation. It is designed to connect everyone and everything including machines, objects and devices for faster and more reliable performance.
** Artificial Intelligence
*** The Internet of Things

YE OLDE SCHOOLHOUSE AND THE SCALLYWAG

Education is a good thing. I've had my share in New York public schools, private universities, company educational facilities, military schools, and the school of hard knocks.

The University of Miami kicked me out in 1957, in my junior year, because I fell behind in paying tuition. I stood in line, in the blazing sun one hot August day to select classes for the next semester. I still owed for the last semester but did not have enough cash to pay. "I'll be able to pay the balance in a few weeks," was my feeble explanation.

The clerk said, "You must pay in full, now." Then, leaning a little to the left, with a dismissive gesture, she called, "Next in line!"

I tried to find out where to go to talk to a higher authority, but it was clear that these lines were for paying customers only.

My plan to pay tuition had been partly based on a 30-day gig as a night janitor at Miami's Bayfront Auditorium. I was scheduled to begin shortly at $1.50 per hour for 40 hours a week.

Tail between my legs I left the area and hiked to the bus stop to catch the first of three buses needed to get to work at the City of Miami's Publicity Department, where I earned $7.50 for three hours of work. That courier job paid $2.50 an hour, a great pay rate, but only 15 or 16 hours per week since it was off the books and paid out of petty cash.

Saturdays were spent doing chores two bus rides away at a nice little Coral Gables apartment complex. There were other little jobs to fill the odd hours. Altogether, around $47.50 a week from the two regular gigs. That would be $469.84 in today's money.

Rent and food cost very little. Cigarettes too much. There was some left over each week for tuition come September. I had almost enough to pay the bill for the previous semester. At about $35.00 per semester hour, a 12-semester-hours program would cost over $4,154.40 in 2022 money. No wonder I was in financial difficulty.

I lost my Student-Deferral Draft Board status on that dreadful day, and realized that I would soon be wearing a uniform.

The University's management of that line was awful. Instead of turning cash-challenged students away completely, they might have referred them to an advisor/advocate to explore other options. I should have gone off to find an advisor on my own but didn't have the energy, sense, or the time, to do it.

Dad was also challenged financially and living in far-off Fort Lauderdale. I didn't want to burden him with my problem. Telephone connections were not like today, where ease of calling almost anywhere, at no cost, did not exist. To talk to him back then, I would need to find a public telephone, after five p.m., and have a pocket full of dimes and quarters.

One fine day after work, walking on Flagler Street in downtown Miami, some weeks after being kicked off the line at the U, I spotted a recruiting poster. Uncle Sam pointed a big forefinger at me and announced, 'Join the Coast Guard Reserve. Six months of active duty for training, and eight years of reserve training.' There was a very cool picture of a 40-foot Coast Guard patrol boat ripping through the waves. No U.S Army for me. I was hooked.

I visited the recruiting office the next day. Took written tests. Gave personal data. Got an eye test and a physical. Pronounced fit, then scheduled to leave, two weeks later, on a morning train for Coast Guard Base, Cape May, New Jersey on November 12, 1957. I could not have imagined what lay ahead.

Coast Guard basic training lasted for 16 intense weeks. The physical and mental aspects were taxing, but I loved it! No worries about where I would sleep. Three squares a day. Structured classes and physical training. Much easier than being a civilian.

Six decades later, I remember my Coast Guard classes more clearly than any from high school or university. One month of training aboard the C.G. Cutter Unimak and finally 30 days of Seamanship School in Groton, Connecticut followed. I was discharged as a Seaman Second Class, E2, 40 pounds heavier than when I got on the train to basic training.

I was able to continue classes at the University of Miami, which was the only college near my Miami, Florida domicile. I found employment at the First National Bank of Miami, married, got out of debt to the college, began to take night classes. Got a B.A. in 1965. Psychology and business management. My wife, my two-year-old son, my dad, and stepmom were in the cheering section.

On off-nights, over an eight-year period. I took classes with the American Institute of Banking and got a lot of good education in the practice of commercial banking.

After graduation from the University of Miami, I was promoted to the rank of Ensign, O-1, in the Coast Guard Reserve and so that became a side-gig for three decades. Over time I attended many weeks of school including the National War College in Norfolk and various naval and Coast Guard schools in Virginia, Rhode Island, and San Francisco. I retired as a commander, O-5, in 1987. My pension started in 1997 on my 60th birthday.

I have taken rewarding classes at several colleges as an adult with no thought of further advancement. Art, photoshop, HTML, printing industry basics, drawing, and such.

My adult jobs in banking, the Coast Guard, and medical administration, food service management, periodical publishing and writing have all been informed by my education both on and off campus.

Damn! What a great country and century to be alive. Even scallywags like me can get ahead.

Great-grand daughter
Isabella Matthews

BILL VERSUS CLAUDINE

I love watching Fareed Zakaria on CNN every Sunday. His balanced reporting on important topics, and his world-class interviews are this news junkie's weekly fix. This week's topics included the social security system and economics.

This essay covers aspects of American life which are, at the end, directly connected to each other. Please join me as I try to stich them together. The following concerns and possible solutions gathered in my mind while watching Fareed yesterday:

1. Social Security.

2. The jobs our economy will be losing.

3. Social Justice.

Social Security.

I've long worried about the imbalance between workers contributing to Social Security and the numbers of retirees drawing benefits. In 1950 the ratio of workers to retiree was about sixteen to one. It is now just two-point-nine workers for each retiree and falling.

This ratio has dropped every year since Social Security's inception in 1937, and we have added new burdens to the system such as Medicare and Medicaid and we have fewer restrictions on who can benefit. The Social Security System's Trust Fund has been merged into the Federal Government's General Account.

Oh dear! Is the sky falling? Soon the system will be bankrupt.

Well, we can and should apply ongoing adjustments such are raising the retirement age and eliminating caps on the income levels the system taxes. We can also increase the SS tax rate and can ease restrictions on immigration (to bolster the number of contributing workers).

There are valid arguments against these proposals but, on balance, the actions proposed should carry any reasoned vote.

These actions cited above will carry the system for decades to come. But soon the number of workers will reduce further.

Then the real fix came to my mind – **workers**. There is a certain irony here but, that's the way it goes.

Workers are more efficient now than they were in middle of the last century. Technology has enabled farmers to produce tons more food with an ever-shrinking number of agro-workers. Same thing in every field of endeavor. Soon we'll be able to produce all our needs with fewer workers.

What will become of the millions of workers whose jobs disappear?

Many Americans will be left behind by great shifts in employment, as happened to over 50 million farmers who were left without work in the mid-20th century, due to increases in productivity. (Think about tractors, harvesters, improved seeds, fertilizers, weather forecasting and other technology.)

Economic depressions, population migration, wars, and great new technology all left their marks on American workers. Many of us will left behind.

While it is true that some American companies use foreign factories to improve profits - the number of jobs lost to technology is much larger. Where are the phone operators, bank tellers and the factories producing books, dictionaries, slide rules, calculators, horse collars, CD players, phonographs, carburetors, film for cameras, cameras, phone books, road maps, and so forth? All gone forever and not shipped overseas.

Reduction in the 40-hour work week, fair tax rates, younger retirement age, realistic minimum wage laws, required community service (Like a draft), and a Guaranteed Minimum Income (GMI) for all members of society are probably in our future. Having a paying job will be a privilege.

Social Justice

I'm a Warren (The Oracle of Omaha) Buffet fan. I recently read an article he wrote for Time Magazine. He stated:

'… A rich family takes care of all its children, not just those with talents valued by the marketplace. … I have no doubt that America can both deliver riches to many and a decent life for all. We must not settle for less.'

The GMI is the alternative to a starving underclass rising up to claim a place. I believe that social justice will have a more attractive price tag than social unrest.

Claudine.

An example of how work is more efficient now than it used to be came to mind when my friend Claudine called me on Saturday. This beautiful Jamaican American woman, a little older than me, called to chat.

We are both members of the Martin Andersen Writers Workshop, and the conversion drifted from talk about other members of the group, to *Chiming of Forgotten Bells*, my recent book.

She mentioned that she was tired out from a trip to her bank. Her Covid mask was uncomfortable, the line was too long, and she could not complete her other errands. And all she needed was to check her balance. She had to go home to rest.

My suggestion that she use her phone for banking fell on rocky ground. "Nooo!" she said, "I am afraid that I'll poosh the wrong boutton and get into trawbol. My seven children and forty-eight grandchildren are not around to help me." Her Jamaican accent was pleasing to my ear.

I was so happy she called. She's a very interesting person, a talented painter about to stage a show, and a good writer with a lot to say. I must mention that her writing is done on a steno pad, and she needs others in the group to transcribe her work into computers – it takes the efforts of two people to get it into our yearly anthology. At least she uses a ball point pen.

Well, you get the point – in five minutes I get more, and better, banking work done with my smart phone than I could have accomplished in half a day when I was working for the largest bank in Florida in the 1960s – a whopping increase in efficiency. There are way fewer bank tellers every year and the number will drop further as we morph into a cashless society.

Not only do I accomplish more, but I also don't stink up the air with auto fumes, I never have a line, never worry about tires, batteries, and accessories, and even avoid late payments – and the many services I receive from the several financial accounts I maintain are free.

There is some irony in the fact that both solutions and problems seem so closely related. Technology both reduces the number of jobs and, at the same time, multiplies our national wealth.

I am hopeful that the future will be better than the past. I'm in good company here, as you will know, if you have read the Peter Diamandis' and Steven Kotler's book, *Abundance: The Future is Better than you Think*. They bring great insight into future technology.

Social justice, global warming – mass human migration, and international cooperation are going to be problems for our grandchildren. *Sorry kids. We did the best we could.*

I am also re-reading *Waldon* and the *Life of Henry David Thoreau*. Henry had terrific ideas about work. He was able to support his simple needs with just a few weeks of paid work as a common laborer each year. He used his 'free time' to communicate with me a century and a half after his death.

AMERICAN RESPONSIBILITY

So, the question was asked, as a prompt, for members of my writing workshop, "Are we responsible for things we should have known?"

Responsibility is often defined in terms of authority and ability to control. A manager should not be held reasonably responsible for events over which she has no authority or influence. There are concepts such as *Unity of Command* and *Span of Control* to be considered.

If an electrical fire burns the house, you probably should not shoot the dog or badmouth your neighbor.

That said, I am a very responsible man. I often shoulder blame for events in my household that are not within my ability to control or for which I did not have the ability to predict. "Bill! " "Daddy!" or "Grandpa!" are often the first words uttered when things go awry. I always rush in to apologize and fix.

Once upon a time ago, I was working as a waiter when a fellow server dropped a glass container of salad dressing, making an oily and broken-glass mess on the floor just inside the servers' ready room. I grabbed a roll of paper towels and a dustpan and began cleaning it up. Thus, I was on my hands scrubbing the floor, with the other servers standing in a circle watching. The culprit was on his way out. Nancy, the manager arrived on the scene and she said, "Billee. I'm agonna whoop yo ass..."

No big deal. I ratted out the offender immediately. I'm now probably the only person in the universe who remembers the incident. What a laugh that was! Blaming the Good Samaritan.

A riff on the question comes to mind – I once had a fundamental Christian friend, named Matt Baker, who asserted that you were sure to go to hell unless you came to Christ. I asked him for a pass for the millions of African and Asian children who, through no fault of their own, would live and die without ever hearing about Jesus. "No exceptions." said Matt. "They're agoin' to Hell."

"What if they live kind and charitable lives and don't sin?"

"Nope. Don't Matter. To hell they go."

Well. I never got Matt to budge an inch but, I've often thought about these matters and I believe in a merciful shepherd, who will make exceptions for critters that stray, for those who were born in the wilderness, and for those who, on balance, were good little lambs even if they do not fear the shepherd's rod and herd dogs.

Another thought is about the term 'Collective Responsibility.' By this I mean to say, "Do we bear responsibility for the sins of our grandfathers who might have been slave owners, oppressors of women's right to vote, or followers of Joseph McCarthy?"

I think that the answer is, "Yes." We should atone for these sins by giving the needy descendants of those harmed a leg up, if necessary, and an acknowledgement of the fact that our society is often wrong about matters.

We are a nation of plenty in a bountiful world in which new technologies often create wealth beyond comprehension. Think about the history of aluminum from precious metal to disposable wrappers for sandwiches and such. Think about the electric power now being created by sun, wind and water - soon to drop in price and become less damaging to our planet.

As a nation of plenty we must share our bounty with those members of our society who can't keep up. We must feed, clothe, house, love and educate them to create a just society. We'll never be perfect, but we must try. Be responsible. Or send shame rather than blessings to future generations.

POLICING AMERICA

Like you, I am disturbed by the news reports of assaults on Americans by our militaristic police and even actual active-duty soldiers. I am intrigued by calls to abolish the police departments in certain cities.

If there were no police, what would protect us from bad and dangerous people? Would we be better off? America did not always have police departments. When the Indians were in charge, they got along without police, as did colonial America.

Policing in Colonial America had been very informal system that employed people part-time. Towns commonly relied on a "night watch" in which volunteers signed up for a certain day and time, mostly to look out for fellow colonists engaging in prostitution or gambling.

I say not Let's not abolish police – let us, instead, make changes that will improve on their stated missions of protection and service.

Here are a few police stats garnered from Wikipedia: 95% of police officers retire without ever drawing their guns. 99% of emergency calls that involve police do not require involve violence.

Yet 100% of police officers are required to wear their guns every day that they are working, even though guns are not necessary. More police officers die as a result of suicide by gun than are killed by violent offenders with weapons.

With the stats in mind, it seems foolish for our country to rely only on a militaristic police force born with guns and clubs. Approaching 100% of the time, negotiating skills, good manners, moral authority, and a commanding presence are all that's needed.

It is just a part of our gun culture that has led us to field armed police that reeks of militarism. Guns do not protect us. They are a threat.

Some say that emergency phone operators might have their beck and call police officers without guns or clubs. Police officers who are trained to deal with situations without violence. Specialized police officers could be summoned who are trained to deal with substance abuse ((alcohol), the homeless, the mentally disturbed, domestic call-outs, and traffic situations.

I would allow police to have guns locked in the trunks of their vehicles to deal with the few times that armed criminals are involved.

America's fixation on guns is a problem which will not be solved anytime soon. But we should start working on it.

The United Kingdom, Norway, New Zealand and a handful of other countries do not rely on armed police. They get along fine and their systems can be studied. Highways in Europe are not patrolled by police looking for speeders – they use roadside cameras to spot and fine offenders.

Note that if your only tool is a hammer, every problem begins looking like a nail. Let us give our emergency call operators a larger variety of tools to deal with caller's problems.

I have had many friends and associates who were police officers. My dear friend **Carmen C.** was a Florida State Trooper on Patrol in the Florida Keys. Patrolling alone, at night, she stopped a speeder. He assaulted her and beat her with her own club-like flashlight while trying to get her gun out of its holster. She resisted and he did not get the gun. He fled, later to be arrested for aggravated assault on a police officer. His female companion was also imprisoned on the same charge.

Carmen was hospitalized with brain damage and had to retire with a disability pension. A few years later the female was up for parole and Carmen traveled from her home in Miami to Tallahassee to testify on her behalf, in the belief that the woman's screaming for the man to stop saved her life.

I think she'd have been better off if her gun had been in the trunk of her cruiser.

My friend, straight shooter, Bob G., a sharp dresser, was an agent for the IRS CID. He was required to carry his weapon. Stopped for reckless speeding on the Florida Turnpike, embarrassed, he did not tell the arresting officer that he was CID. Taken to jail to appear before a magistrate, he was sitting in a holding cell with a bunch of toughs and suddenly realized that he had forgotten to tell the arresting officials that he was wearing a gun under his suit jacket. Panic.

He got the attention of a jailer and whispered his secret. Totally embarrassing himself and his jailers. He was let off by a kind judge with a simple speeding fine and never mentioned the matter to his superiors.

The only other police gun story I'll tell here is about my pal **Arnold L.'s** scary crawl through a laundry's back window on a cold, dark New England night – the open alley window made him think that a crime was in process. He quietly entered the building through the open window, tiptoed into a hallway with his gun in one hand, his flashlight in the other, and his heart in his mouth.

He sensed a presence. He whirled to face it, turning his flashlight on. There was a burly guy standing there pointing a gun at Arnold. Arnold fired a volley and discovered his assailant to be his own image reflected by a large, now fractured mirror. There was no intruder.

I think these episodes reveal that a gun is not always a police officer's best tool.

NOW AND THEN
PROBLEMATIC ISSUES AND SOLUTIONS
HATE AND FORGIVENESS

I confess that I have been reading Henry David Thoreau (1817-1872), as well as a biography about his life. I am in awe of his brilliance and how much he accomplished in his scant 55 years.

In a seemingly casual style, he affected the thoughts of millions regarding freedom versus slavery, the effect of man upon the climate, the extinction of species, the dignity of work and leisure, civil disobedience and the importance of living simply. Every sentence he wrote is fraught with learning and a push for change in the reader.

What a guy!

I too wish for a better world, but I don't want to give up my computer, my smart phone, air conditioning, electric lights, indoor plumbing and, of course my beloved flat-screen T.V. I am musing about how things are today versus in historical times.

So, I set my pen to paper and my mind to work on problems and solutions. Mostly I am thinking about the United States.

RACISM 1920 vs. 2020. Fewer lynchings now. The protection of law has expanded, but we still have much work to do. The right of the people for peaceably assemble and petition the government for redress of grievances is chiseled in stone in the U.S. Constitution's Bill of Rights.

SOCIAL JUSTICE 1820 vs. 2020. Slavery is dead. Adults of any sex or race vote. Might we all have equal rights to education, housing, clothing, food, clean air and water, basic income; or are these rights abridged if we are born to poor mothers?

PRODUCTIVITY AND EFFICIENCY 1720 vs. 2050. It's a double-edged sword. When machinery and computers eliminate jobs. And when our country can produce way more than we need with far fewer workers. When might there very few jobs available? Can A.I. eliminate managers, professionals, and innovators, as well as ordinary wage earners?

THE NATIONAL DEBT 1945 vs. 2021. Today's worries will be forgotten. So, what if we owe a year's GNP? If we use the money to achieve social justice, we'll save big on prisons, police and health.

IMMIGRATION 1620 vs. 2020. We'd better keep the door open, be willing to evolve and love our fellow man. American's reputation is on the line. Are we a force for good or evil?

THE AMERCAN JUSTICE SYSTEM 1520 vs. 2020. The U.S. has more prisoners than any other country in the world. Native American peoples had no prisons. Can we learn from them? Could some of our laws be flawed? The answer is obvious - quit locking people up unless they are an immediate threat to others. Heal and rehabilitate rather than punish.

CLIMATE CHANGE 1816 vs. 2020. In 1816 (The year without a summer) Global temps dropped 1.5 degrees Fahrenheit. World-wide harvests were reduced by freezing weather in mid-summer. Volcanic activity put sun-blocking dust in the air and disrupted crops for two years – this caused much hardship and shifting of populations.

TERRORISM 2000 vs. 2020. Many things have changed for Americans. Some say that we are the terrorists, manufacturing bombs and other weapons for the world. And that our armed police and populace are too dangerous.

POVERTY 2020 vs. 2025. Worldwide trends are shifting people, by the hundreds of millions, out of profound poverty. If this trend continues the world will be a better and healthier place for mankind. Studies show that the direct giving of cash to poor people is the better way,
ELDERLY CARE 2020 vs. 2030. I can't think about this. I love where I'm at and I wish the same for everyone.
PUBLIC HEALTH 1920 vs. 2120. We'll live longer, work more efficiently, end world hunger and achieve peace for all.

The list is not complete, nor are my thoughts fully expressed or evolved. The items are not presented in the order of importance I give to each subject. Henry is whirling in his grave, trying to get some answers out to us.
Forgiveness, I think, is the greatest element for positive change.

MAGIC IS IN THE AIR

In Arthur C. Clarke's book *3001*, he made a very interesting point. He said that a man from the year 1000 would regard today's technology as magic.

In the same vein, I believe that he also said that the technology in the year 3000 will seem like magic to a person from our era.

Much of the technology that I'm using today seems like pure magic to the 1940's boy that is still inside my head. I do things that I couldn't have conceived of when I was a young man. For example, I use my phone to take pictures, as a photo album, as a calculator, as a means of receiving and sending messages and mail, for navigation in any part of the world, as a flashlight, alarm clock, dictionary, phone book, newspaper, calendar, weather report source, and much more. Perhaps, the most drastic thing of all is that I have given away all my books to local libraries.

A few books have been kept for decoration and sentimental purposes, however there are thousands, perhaps millions, of volumes in my pocket, on my phone, ready to read at my pleasure.

I usually read three or four books at the same time: fiction in the morning, history in the afternoon, and maybe a little philosophy toward the end of the day. My faithful *friend* always bookmarks the last page read so I don't get confused.

When my wife and I go on a trip we no longer pack any books. Zero! We just load the books that we plan to read into the phone and go off on our trip never missing a lick. I read the New York Times and my local paper every day, even while tripping.

Furthermore, if some interesting reading opportunity occurs to us, even in the middle of the ocean, we download the appropriate tome and become instant experts in arcane subjects.

I'm sorry to say that I don't borrow books from the library anymore. It's easier and cheaper to buy them from Kindle.

People tell me that they like the look and feel of a book and would miss it terribly if they couldn't hold a paper book. I, on the other hand, now like the look and feel of my phone. It's so light. I like it smooth, warm surface. I like the way it smells. Beyond that, I like that I can look up words I don't understand immediately, without interrupting my reading. Interesting bits and articles can easily be shared with friends. Maps can instantly appear to give a look at the geography of a 'read.'

We got a new TV. It's a smart one it's twice as big as the Old 40-incher. It does lots of tricks. Thank Heaven we had our grandchildren to set it up and explain the magic.

Oh, and I forgot to say that I dictated these musings and printed them without the use of wire connections, from my phone to your computer, and finally to the pages of *This Is Not A Book.*

As the wise man said, "Gee whiz – It's magic!"

IF I WERE KING

I dream of a system where it would be impossible for people to vote in more than one state or jurisdiction.

That system would erase gerrymandering, voter disenfranchisement, and claims of voter fraud by sore losers. One person. One vote!

And I would require all eligible voters to vote. A fine of $100.00 for failure to vote might be enough to stir a lazy voter to do her civic duty. Australia fines non-voters $55.00 (Australian) and I confess, that is where I got the idea.

Our social security numbers can be linked to facial ID, fingerprint ID or other means and each state would make its own rules.

In case you were wondering, out wonderful social security numbering system has about one billion possible combinations and it should be good for many decades to come. Tech is quickly making old-fashioned methods of identification obsolete.

I dream of a system where each American's vote has equal value. Presently, it is entirely possible that a person getting fewer votes than his opponent. Remember 2000 and 2016 when that happened? My vote didn't count as much as it should have.

Our system is truly great, but, even so, it can use a tweak or two. I say, let's start with the elimination of the Electoral College. I think we can trust a congressional committee to accept, tabulate and certify the number of votes for each candidate. We should not let each state have the right to cast their votes for a single candidate.

If each state manages election matters differently, within federal guidelines of course, we are safer from foreign interference as it will be harder for a computer hacker to attack many different systems rather than just one big one. And we will have to sharpen our defenses for future elections

If I were king, that's what I would do.

Any questions? Put your right hand on the chopping block and close your eyes.

UNEMPLOYED FOR 21 YEARS

I wondered what I could write about for tomorrow's workshop. Turns out I'm concerned about unemployment. No, silly. Not about what work I should be doing, but about what work my great grandchildren will have available. Say in the year 2050.

This cartoon greeted me this morning in my digital copy of the Daytona Beach News Journal. It sealed the deal. I decided to write about future unemployment.

OLIVER TWIST, CIRCA 2021

MIKE THOMPSON/USA TODAY NETWORK

Jobs are now disappearing at an alarming rate. Bank tellers, cashiers, cab drivers, surgeons, pilots, ship captains, teachers, mechanics and many, many occupations will be affected. Automation, modern innovation and efficiency will eliminate more jobs soon.

Consider auto mechanics. Electric cars have about one hundred moving parts in their power plants. This compares to four hundred or so in modern gasoline or diesel engines. This will not only affect automobile manufacturing but also auto mechanics whose jobs will be easier and require different skills.

Not only self-driving automobiles but pilot-less planes, captain-less ships, and shipping containers that will move much more efficiently from the place they were packed to the place where they will be unloaded. Jobs will be lost.

So, is 'job loss' a bad thing or good thing? Or some of each.

I don't know for sure but consider the fable island with ten men and ten women in the tiny tribe. The men fished and the women worked on land. They were happy and self-sufficient.

Then the unthinkable happened. A ship stopped by and gifted them with a net. Now one fisherman could supply the needs of the tribe and nine others could sit on the beach and watch. OMG – is the tribe better off?

I believe it is better off because the nine unemployed could turn their minds to other matters such as learning how to build better shelters and boats, or perhaps a way to preserve the catch so that the remaining fisherman will have to work even fewer days each week. He too then will then have leisure to think about how to improve their island world. I hope they would not stigmatize the unemployed.

What are we to do with the unemployed truck drivers, cab drivers, Uber drivers airplane pilots, ship captains, lawyers, teachers and the stevedores and longshoremen who used to work with shipping containers? They and the cashiers, bank tellers, hotel desk clerks and so many other jobless people will be sitting 'on the beach.' Are we better off?

I think we are better off *only* if we establish the right to a comfortable and safe life for all our people – that means a guaranteed minimum income for everyone. I know it sounds like communism but if we preserve private ownership rights and the entrepreneurship of our population many new jobs will be created.

Even if we are not able to replace all jobs and unemployment is impossible to eliminate, we should not stigmatize people who do not work.

Consider an unwed mother with two or three small children and no support from the father or fathers. She would find it very difficult to work in a low-income job because she could not afford childcare. Should her children be punished? Is the hand that rocks the cradle not valuable? Let's not allow such mothers to live in poverty. I think not, not, not!

Warren Buffett famously said that a wealthy family will take care of all its children regardless of their ability to contribute financially to the family's wealth. In the same way in a wealthy country should take care of all its people, regardless of their ability to contribute.

Of those people who do not work, consider that they might use their leisure to educate themselves or perhaps to author silly essays like this. I am unemployed. I cannot work because I am somewhat disabled by age. Do you want me to live in poverty?

The great efficiencies that will come in manufacturing, transport, education, and other facets of our society will create wealth for the nation in ways that we cannot now calculate. I say we must use that wealth for good purposes.

I know there are facets of the subject that I have not examined, and that 'economics' is complex. I have just hit upon a few of the many factors in play.

I am reminded by my writing friend Tom Kramer that the face of poverty is female. Young, and perhaps unwed, mothers are more likely to live in poverty than the fathers of their children. Impoverished children suffer in many ways including health and education. Being less fit for life, such young people are more likely to be incarcerated, in ill health, and psychologically damaged.

I will shout out that the hand that rocks the cradle is as deserving of a good life as the working person with no children. Such women can't afford the expense of childcare and are hobbled and despised in the job marketplace.

When I was a working man, I loved my jobs. Now that I am retired, I seriously enjoy not having to work for a living.

I dropped out early, way before I had to, so I was a burden on society. Not wealthy in cash assets alone, Daisy and I were rich in having two Social Security pensions plus two modest pensions and a little investment income. We are fortunate.

My wish for you is that you can always do work that you love. Or be able to have a good life even if you are caring for your children.

HUMAN CAPITAL

I read an amazing New York Times opinion piece by Nicholas Kristof, the Pulitzer Prize-winning columnist; now retired, and a candidate for the governor of Oregon. I'd vote him in a heartbeat.

It was his farewell to journalism giving a glowing salute to the New York Times for 25 wonderful years. He wrote about the terrible happenings he covered in Bosnia and Darfur – events involving genocide, mass starvation and unspeakable horrors of war.

His take-away from years in these conflicts was very positive. He mentioned three life lessons:

Lesson One. Side by side with the worst of humanity, you will find the best.

Lesson Two. We largely know how to improve well-being at home and abroad. What we lack is the political will.

Lesson thre. Talent is universal, even if opportunity is not.

Some examples he cited were the side-by-side increases in human longevity, the lowering of birth-rates and reductions of profound poverty on earth. He illustrated these lessons with examples from his own experience and made me a believer.

My take-away from his fine column is that we need to know there are brilliant leaders, statesmen, inventors and future statesmen in the genes of the hordes of wretched humans at the borders of our various successful countries. We must find a way to give them opportunity.

It was once unthinkable that a Catholic or an Irishman could be elected president. People of color were not even considered for the football positions of quarterback for head coach. *They lacked intelligence.*

So, I gets to thinking, *What shall I write about for Monday's meeting of The Ormand Writers Workshop?* Then came thoughts about individuals who have contributed mightily to our well-being and safety.

Jesus Christ, Mohammed,
Gandhi, the Dali Llama   Peace and love
        Alexander Hamilton   Good governance
Mahatma Gandhi and Nelson,
        Mandela   Peace and forgiveness
Jeanne of Arc   Courage is universal
Abraham Lincoln   The Emancipation
                                              Proclamation

John Crapper   Flush toilets
Marie Cure   Xray
Thomas Edison   Chased out the night
Ottmar Mergenthaler   Linotype
Queen Elizabeth   English Culture
William Cullen   Refrigeration
Willis Carrier   Air conditioning
Franklyn D. Roosevelt   Social Security
Jonas Salk   Polio Vaccine
Dwight D. Eisenhower   Interstate Highways

Lyndon Johnson	Medicare
European Statesmen	European Union
Mother Theresa	Love for the poor
Gloria Steinman	Women's Rights
Mark Zuckerberg	Facebook
Jeff Bezos	Amazon
Many clever individuals	Internal Combustion Engines, Automatic transmissions, Pneumatic tires, Cathode Ray Tubes, Television, Computers, Solid-state diodes, GPS systems, iPhones, etc.

I hope that you will add to the list and correct me where I err. These men and women have wildly different origins and financial birth circumstances.

That brings me back to the point I want to make. Human capital is valuable and not to be wasted by allowing children to grow in poverty or denied educational opportunities.

Time's a wasting! United States Homeland Security Department and Immigration and Customs Enforcement Agency. Let's get out the visa forms and start following the law.

DEFINING OUR RIGHTS

I read the digital New York Times every day on my smartphone. Oftentimes, stories are deeply disturbing and make me think how lucky I am to be an elderly, white, retired, married male in the United States of America in this, the year of our Lord, 2021.

A brilliant story in today's paper moved me to think about Human Rights. I made a list that included clean air, clean water, food security, shelter, security, education, and freedom.

The story was about the actions of our government in rounding up, and forcibly deporting people, and even preventing refugees from reaching our border to plea for asylum.

As I contemplated my list, I realized that there were other rights, equally important, that should be listed under the major headings for example under Shelter – sanitation systems, refrigeration and privacy might be added, and under Freedom we could put the rights of family under Security we could include financial security under that perhaps minimum wage.

This is what the list looks like, ordered like a chart, with some subheadings:CLEAN AIR
No smoky heating or indoor
cooking fires.

CLEAN WATER
In the house

FOOD SECURITY

SHELTER
Sanitation Systems
Privacy
Refrigeration

SECURITY
Financial Security
Decent minimum wage

EDUCATION AND OPPORTUNITY

FREEDOM
Freedom from unreasonable
family separations
From unreasonable search or intrusion

(The above is abbreviated. My detailed list would be longer)

Well, having these rights is one thing. Another thing entirely is guaranteeing that happens Whose job is that? I say that should be a primary function of government to work on securing Human Rights for all.

Today's disturbing story was a long report on capturing illegal immigrants near the Mexican border in Southern California. It included the plight of Juan Carreras.*

He is the owner of a business in southern California. He and his wife have five young children. They own a nice home with a swimming pool and other amenities. They were ideal citizens except for one thing. Juan is an undocumented immigrant.

He came to this country, a Mexican citizen from Guanajuato, Mexico, over 20 years ago and began working to achieve a decent lifestyle. He married a woman who had a child from previous marriage, and they had four children together.

He fell afoul of the law for a traffic infraction and thus came to the attention of ICE. Juan was easily captured and expelled to Mexico. His wife and children are American citizens, but their breadwinner and heart of the family had to go – a heartbreaking situation.

He tried to reenter again illegally was charged jailed for the crime of illegally entering the country. He was released from jail and returned to Mexico and, desperate to get back to his children, he again broke the law. There was no other path for him to follow.

Seems to me that exceptions could and should be made to our immigration laws policies and practices in cases like Juan's. There *oughta* be a law that no person may be deported without a judicial hearing whose sole purpose is to ensure that the government works for the greatest good.

The Constitution and Bill of Rights do not only refer to citizens. They speak of Persons, and I say that Juan is definitely a person. If I were his Judge I'd make an exception. If I were a law enforcement officer I would make an exception. There are plenty of bad guys to work on. We don't need to grab fathers off of the street and send them to hell.

***

There are hundreds of millions of people around the world who do not have basic human rights – for example Shelter – too many of us need to defecate on the ground without even a hint of privacy or sanitary supplies. Hundreds of millions of people don't have a water source readily available. For them, Food security and Shelter Security are absent. Their rights to an education and the freedom to pursue happiness are nonexistent. I think that we should ensure that every person within our borders has basic human rights and that should be the primary focus of our government. We should be an example to the world.

We are so focused on maintaining an invincible army to conquer anybody who might threaten our country, that we spend trillions of dollars on that, and **not nearly enough** to ensure that children born into poor families have healthcare, financial security, and the right to pursue happiness. They grow up locked in the battle to survive.

*Juan CARRERAS IS NOT HIS REAL NAME.

***

HERE IS THE ARTICLE AND A LINK IF YOU'D LIKE TO READ IT FOR YOURSELF. IT IS A LONG READ AND PLEASE DO NOT FEEL THAT YOU MUST DO SO. IT IS MY INTENTIONTHAT THE ESSAY ABOVE STAND ALONE ON MY BLOG.

https://www.nytimes.com/2021/02/03/magazine/customs-border-protection-migrants-pacific-ocean.html?referringSource=articleShare

The fiberglass skiff Lazora idled on the darkened Pacific Ocean a few miles south of American waters. It was roughly 25 feet long and seven feet wide, unlit, overloaded and offering no shelter from the elements. Twenty people were crammed aboard. Most were seated on narrow benches. A few huddled on the vomit-splattered deck. Some had opened slits in plastic garbage bags and pushed heads and arms through, flimsy protection against the damp October chill. Few life jackets were visible. At the boat's stern, two Mexican men tended a 200-horsepower outboard engine and 10 plastic barrels of fuel. They were in the final hour of ferrying a load of undocumented migrants toward American land, in waters nearly three-quarters of a mile deep: human smugglers, running a boat through a seam where black sea met black sky.

The boat operators, one a former commercial fisherman and the other his cousin, had picked up their passengers earlier in the night on a beach on Mexico's coastline and worked their way offshore and northward. Shortly after midnight they arrived at a de facto loitering zone for maritime smugglers preparing for runs into the United States, a patch of ocean just south of the American line where Mexican law-enforcement vessels rarely patrol, and American vessels have no authority.

Now their uneventful ride was giving way to tension and fear.

The lights of San Diego and Tijuana twinkled in the eastern distance. The Lazora's destination was the steep outcropping of Point Loma, beside the entrance to San Diego's harbor, where the men running the skiff had been told a pickup crew would guide them to the beach with a flashing light. From there the migrants were expected to follow a Southern California human-smuggling routine — a leap into the surf, a scramble ashore, a rush to waiting vehicles, a drive to safe houses where they would be held until the balance of their smuggling fees had been paid. And then, if it all worked, if no one drowned, if the ever-shifting network of federal, state and municipal law-enforcement agencies did not catch them, they would embark on a furtive form of opportunity in the United States.

They came from multiple Mexican states and matched familiar profiles of undocumented migrants seeking to cross. One was a 56-year-old widower from Colima who supported three children and two grandchildren. Another was a young man from Nayarit who cared for a mother sick with cancer. A teenage minor was among them, as was a man from Oaxaca who turned 18 two weeks earlier and wanted a job. A 41-year-old man from Michoacan had boarded the skiff to seek reunion with his daughter, who preceded him to the United States with hopes of studying in an American school.

Huddled in the bow was a man who fit a less familiar but not uncommon profile — a Mexican citizen from Guanajuato who for more than two decades had lived and worked in the United States. (To protect him and his family, he is referred to here as J., one of his initials.) Under the law, J. was not just attempting a single illegal entry. He was a recidivist, a serial border-tester. He had a wife with whom he had been raising five American children near a Western American city, where he owned a landscaping and gardening business until he was seized and deported by Immigration and Customs Enforcement in 2018, amid the Trump administration's wider crackdown on immigration and undocumented residents in the United States. For two years he had been living an odyssey of his times. Unwillingly estranged from his family, he was trying to return to the single-story duplex with a swimming pool in the back where his wife and children were waiting, including a stepdaughter he had encouraged to attend college and four biological American children of his own. J. was journeying home.

For almost three hours the Lazora had been milling near the international boundary, driving this way then that, its crew seemingly unsure when to commit. It was almost as if they knew that a Customs and Border Protection airplane with an infrared sensor had been circling overhead, and that the sensor operator, seated behind the pilots, was watching them on a dimly illuminated black-and-white display. It was 2:45 a.m. The law-enforcement aircraft was low on fuel. It would soon return to its airfield, potentially leaving two 41-foot C.B.P.

Coastal Interceptor Vessels, each crewed by interdiction agents, without a plane to scan the expansive ocean surface and guide them to their quarry. "Targets," they called boats like the Lazora.

The enforcement vessels were now drifting quietly inside American waters about 12 miles away, lights out, engines warm and murmuring, ready.

The men at the skiff's stern decided. The former fisherman spun the throttle, accelerating past 20 knots.

The nighttime run of the Lazora, late in 2019, was but one moment in an oceanic human-smuggling pipeline that grew in volume during the administration of President Donald J. Trump, part of a border-policy-and-enforcement puzzle President Joseph R. Biden Jr. inherits. Cross-border human smuggling at sea has a long history, on California's coast as elsewhere, and smuggling here rose sharply more than a decade ago. That increase was driven in part by the installation of more fences and sensors on land borders but also by a tourism

decline in Baja California as Mexico, gripped by cartel wars, became more dangerous. Lean economic conditions encouraged idled laborers and fishermen, some who used to guide visiting anglers and scuba divers, to work in drug- and human-smuggling rackets. For years the transits have mostly relied on simple, flat-bottomed fishing skiffs with sharp bows, known as pangas, that are well suited for beach launches and landings. Pleasure craft, often stolen, are also involved. The authorities in Southern California have caught almost 6,700 people since late 2009 entering American territory by water; about one-fifth of those were apprehended last year.

Law-enforcement encounters with migrants at sea subsided late in the Obama administration but never stopped, and the authorities say traffic increased anew as boat smuggling became more lucrative in a climate of tighter land-border enforcement under President Trump. The smuggling rings now carry residents from far beyond Mexico, including people from China and Yemen as well as multiple South and Central American countries, who travel to Mexico and seek the services of "coyotes" who arrange illegal trips for fees. Agents say the arrival of migrants from distant countries is readily explicable: Intensified screening to board commercial airliners overseas and at passport control at American airports has led people from other hemispheres to try the Baja-to-San Diego small-boat run.

To deter incursions, the Coast Guard and Customs and Border Protection cooperate on the water in counter smuggling surveillance and patrols, part of a collaboration with federal, state, and local law-enforcement agencies. Integration is necessary, officials from both agencies say, because migrants on a smuggling boat that reaches shore pass through multiple jurisdictions, and varied law-enforcement agencies have different equipment and capabilities as well as distinct responsibilities, ultimately including housing and deporting people who are detained.

For Customs and Border Protection, ocean enforcement in Southern California falls to the San Diego office of the Air and Marine Operations branch, an organization that nationally operates roughly 300 vessels and 240 aircraft, including Black Hawk helicopters and Predator drones. The militarization of the agency predates the Trump administration. C.B.P. received its first 41-foot Coastal Interceptor Vessel in 2016, before Trump won the election; the first Super King Air Multi-Role Enforcement Aircraft, the type that flew over the Lazora, were fielded years earlier.

Given the agency's reliance on equipment identical or similar to that in military service, it is unsurprising that the branch relies on veterans of the armed forces to fill its ranks. Sixty-two percent of its agents have previous military service. On the aviation side, many C.B.P. pilots and sensor operators are retirees with thousands of hours of flight experience, from transport helicopters to fighter jets. Many agents on the water previously served in the Navy, Marines or Coast Guard. To meet infrastructure needs, the agency is also in part geographically grafted onto Coast Guard and military installations: In San Diego, C.B.P. aircraft fly from a naval air base; its boats tie off at Navy, Marine and Coast Guard docks.

The Air and Marine Operations branch is one set of gears in a sprawling system, and enforcement efforts near San Diego cover a tiny portion of a national border that is porous in many places and ways. Agents in aircraft and boats have almost no influence over national policy or the practices of other agencies in the Department of Homeland Security and Department of Justice, including Immigration and Customs Enforcement, U.S. attorneys' offices and the Bureau of Prisons — organizations whose actions can create shifts in the cat-mouse encounters at sea. Changes in policy or police actions in Mexico also influence smugglers' behaviors, another factor in an immigration puzzle that no presidential administration or law-enforcement agency has been able to solve.

The puzzle is complicated enough to defy intuition. Increased emphasis on enforcement, for example, has not necessarily resulted in decreased smuggling traffic. In the last year of President Trump's term, Southern California experienced the busiest maritime smuggling year on record, so much so that the 1,273 apprehensions of migrants trying to reach the region by sea in fiscal 2020 almost quintupled those of the last year of the Obama administration. Agents attribute the surge to stricter land-border enforcement and perhaps to border closures during the coronavirus pandemic. The fast pace has continued into 2021, including 35 apprehensions in a single weekend in January. Agents anticipate another uptick as smugglers and migrants, aware of the Biden administration's desire to reduce deportations during an immigration-policy review, test enforcement while the country's border posture changes yet again.

As marine agents patrolled that fall, J. made up his mind: He would try to enter the United States by sea — a decision drawn by his arrest on two previous tries to cross the land border in 2018. J. was in his 40s and came to the United States in the 1990s. His brother also entered and had become a naturalized citizen, a status that allowed their mother to arrive legally in 2002 and naturalize in 2014.

As part of a family straddling two nations, in and out of compliance with immigration law, J.'s life blended success with struggles. He married a woman in the United States who was also an undocumented immigrant from Mexico and became stepfather to her young daughter, who had been born in the United States. The couple had four more children, all born American citizens. He owned and ran a landscaping business, and the family lived in a small home a short drive from the public school the children attended. J. also had run-ins with the law, including a misdemeanor conviction for obstructing a police officer in 2001 and two misdemeanor convictions of driving under the influence of alcohol, one in 2004 and another in 2016. For the last conviction, he was sentenced to 15 days in jail and three years of probation. Probationary status brought J. to the attention of Immigration and Customs Enforcement, according to a law-enforcement report and Emerson Wheat, one of the lawyers who has represented him. In 2018, ICE opened what it called a "fugitive operation" and sought J.'s arrest.

As a busy father and business owner, J. kept a routine. He was not hard to trace. Three of his children attended the same school, and he drove them there in his silver Chrysler 300 at the same time each day, facts readily available to ICE, which put his home under surveillance.

One school day J. woke and prepared his children breakfast, as was his habit, his stepdaughter says. At about 8:30 a.m., he loaded his children into the car and took them to school. Two deportation officers in plain clothes followed in an unmarked vehicle. At the school, J. escorted one of his daughters, a kindergartner, to her classroom. The deportation officers took him into custody after he returned to his car. While being arrested, J. tossed his keys to a client of his gardening business, who tried to intervene.

His stepdaughter, then in high school, was in class when she heard something was awry. Her mother called before lunch, she says, to tell her J. had not returned. "Where could he be?" her mother asked. She called again at lunchtime to say she had still not heard from him. Shortly before the school day's last bell, her mother phoned with news: ICE had taken J. "He just called me," she said. For a moment, his stepdaughter recalls, she felt as if time no longer moved. She rushed home to find her mother screaming; her grandmother told her to pick up the other children. The family protected the kids from hearing of their father's arrest until his case made local news. His youngest daughter, the kindergartner, saw the report. She asked: "Why is my dad on TV?"

Without J.'s income, his family's resources dwindled. His stepdaughter took on two jobs — working at Olive Garden and at a carwash — to help their mother keep their home. J. tried fighting the case, but against an assertive government, his position was weak. In autumn 2018, federal agents returned him to Mexico through the border crossing at San Ysidro, Calif., with a warning not to return.

Expulsion did not deter J.'s desire to be with his family. "The best way I can describe it is that your heart does not get deported with you," says Wheat, who took on J.'s case after his return to Mexico. "It's a magnet, and it draws you back." Less than a week after being repatriated, J. scaled a border fence east of Calexico, Calif. A federal agent apprehended him. He was processed and swiftly returned over the border. This new encounter with the authorities also did not dissuade him. J. had a relative in Mexicali, a Mexican border city. There he met a coyote who agreed to provide him an American birth certificate, issued to a citizen of his age with the surname Paez, with which to try crossing into the United States officially. He was to pay $7,000 if successful.

About five weeks later J. walked into the Calexico Point of Entry and presented the birth certificate for admission as German Paez. C.B.P. agents detained him on the spot. His fingerprints revealed his real identity, along with his criminal and immigration history. J. was charged with a felony — misuse of an entry document — and served 85 days in jail until being granted supervised release. Again the government returned him to Mexico.

He turned his attention to a passage by sea. By fall 2019, he had made contact with coyotes who organized panga runs and notified his family of the plan. The fee was to be $10,000, his stepdaughter says, payable upon arrival. The smugglers assured him the panga would have life jackets and had him wait in a house in Baja. His family was nervous, and not just about the ocean journey. J. has diabetes, and his health had been failing, his stepdaughter says. From his relatives' perspective, it was past time for him to be home, living in the care of his American family. But the way was guarded and the route uncertain.

While many smuggling runs are sprints through near-shore waters, panga transits from a launch in Baja to the California coast can consume hours or even days. This is because some vessels stop at the Coronado Islands, inside Mexican territory, to load barrels of fuel. Others swing far to sea before turning north and crossing what the authorities call the "maritime boundary line," or M.B.L. Still others rendezvous with a refueling boat before for the run. Some nights smugglers coordinate in tactics that leverage the speed and maneuverability of small craft, including in two-vessel incursions in which one boat will attract law enforcement so a second boat can follow. "Whenever I see someone inside, I look out further to see what else is coming," Detection Enforcement Officer Ned Leonard said, as he flew in an aviation patrol over the ocean in late 2019. Sometimes, he said, he spots decoys. "The other night I saw a Jet Ski hanging just below the M.B.L., waiting to draw out law enforcement."

Before joining the C.B.P. in 2009, Leonard operated sensors in the Navy's E-2C Hawkeye, a surveillance and command-and-control aircraft with a massive, disc-shaped radome. The plane in which he flew now — a Super King Air turboprop — also makes for a strange sight. With a radar pod bulging on its underside and a pair of stabilizing strakes aft to reduce yaw, it looks like an aeronautical engineer's flirtation with a flightless bird. These aircraft take off from Naval Air Station North Island most days, turn south and scan their unblinking digital eyes across the waters, trying to sift smuggling craft from the rest. To do so they train lenses on each vessel and make a judgment based on what can be seen of the boat's cargo or discerned from its behavior. Sensor operators are familiar with common headings to and from fishing spots in

Mexico, as well as routes for aquaculture boats from Baja's ports to bluefin-tuna pens south of the border. They also know the frequently used jumping-off points for smuggling boats, including a marina at which the manager was killed in 2019 in what agents deemed a smuggling-related murder. "Cartels are fighting over this space," Leonard said.

On this night many boats below moved according to patterns. At the displays, Leonard narrated into a microphone for pilots in the cockpit. Gulls swarmed around one boat. "It's a good indicator that they are fishing," he said. He toggled the sensors to another.

Below him, a pair of pangas appeared. They were heading northeast from offshore fishing grounds toward Ensenada, heavy with bundled nets. The wind was blowing chop across a moderate swell. Even loaded with gear and, presumably, catch, they zipped along at 27 knots, bounding and slamming into waves as they beat their way to port. This kind of speed can be decisive. When winds subside and seas go calm, a panga crowded with migrants and pushed by the 200-horsepower Yamaha outboards common to Baja's fleets can cruise at more than 30 knots, slipping past the authorities and quickly hitting drop-off points.

Enforcement difficulties are compounded by gaps in patrol schedules. The Super King Air is almost all-seeing, and when paired with an Interceptor vessel it can direct agents to suspicious boats. But C.B.P. staff is too small to patrol round the clock. Moreover, C.B.P. aircraft fly from a prominent airfield, and Interceptor vessels dock at piers visible from San Diego and terrain nearby. It is an article of faith among agents that smugglers deploy spotters who relay the agents' movements. "We are confident that they are watching us take off, or know when we are flying," says Air Interdiction Agent Troy Fuller, a pilot who formerly flew Marine Corps helicopters. Chad Irick, a supervisory agent and former Army Apache pilot, believes the smugglers have even more information. "They definitely know our shifts, they know what our response times are and they have spotters out," he says.

Agents also say they have seen indications of real-time smugglers' communications. Sometimes they are told a vessel in Mexico is approaching and rush from their docks to intercept it, only to have the boat turn around as an enforcement vessel roars out of the harbor. The phenomenon is common enough to have a shorthand expression: T.B.S., for "turned back south." Leonard said agents suspect smugglers pass alerts on marine-band radio. "The smugglers get on Channel 16 when they know a plane is in the air and whistle or say, 'la mosca,'" he said, Spanish for "the fly."

During the years of anti-immigration populism that accompanied Trumpism — with its racist tropes, calls to build more border walls and news reports of migrants or undocumented residents suffering in the immigration crackdown — agents say they have at times felt social disapproval. Some say they hesitate to wear uniforms when commuting or do not tell neighbors what they do for work. Others describe being confronted when ordering food in restaurants or by passers-by at docks, including by a small crowd that called agents "Nazis" as they detained a suspected smuggler at the waterfront Pepper Park in 2018. The unease is also informed by the 2017 shooting of an Air and Marine Operations agent in a C.B.P. uniform outside a Florida grocery store by an 18-year-old man who said he hated cops; the agent, shot five times, survived.

Even as public tensions have accompanied enforcement, Southern California has experienced a rise in boat-smuggling traffic and migrant drownings, all but ensuring those tensions will continue. Agents know they don't detect all the smugglers, much less catch them. Sometimes abandoned boats are found at sunrise, tied to a harbor dock or banging in the surf; other times, Border Patrol agents are called to collect life preservers, swim noodles, boogie boards or swim fins on beaches, discarded by migrants who made it. Occasionally smugglers game out the gaps in C.B.P. shifts and dare daylight dashes. Soon after Leonard's evening flight, which was quiet, a panga made a fast passage to Point Loma, dropped passengers in the water and spun around. A Black Hawk helicopter gave chase. But no Interceptor vessel was on the water, and the man easily sped out of U.S. territory — a successful run, at least for him. The migrants he ferried were detained ashore.

The full extent of traffic remains unknowable. Agents note that enforcement data principally reflects events in which a vessel is recovered or people detained; it offers little insight into undetected passages. Shifts in data over time, they say, may be tied to some degree to shifts in enforcement capabilities and efforts, like the arrival of the Super King Air aircraft. Mark Levan, a supervisory agent who has worked the waters since 2002, says there is no solid information on how many boats and migrants get through, but the activity is rising. "We're catching more than we ever caught, but it's not slowing down," he says. Levan is nearing retirement. His government career reaches back to service in the Navy in the 1980s, including alongside Marines in Beirut. He speaks of Baja's human-smuggling rackets in the knowing tone of someone who has tried for years to counter networks that not only defied crackdowns but thrived.

The smugglers, he says, follow a rational risk assessment. Pangas can carry people or drugs. But penalties for ferrying migrants are lesser than for trafficking drugs, so panga crews prefer to smuggle people. "Boat drivers get a quarter of the time if they're moving bodies, as opposed to dope," he says, referring to prison sentences. The fees migrants are willing to pay have also climbed, Levan says, making smuggling an understandable temptation. Prices vary, but Levan says each migrant now pays $10,000 or more for the passage, up from $6,000 a few years ago and far more than when Levan started in his job. (These rates were confirmed by lawyers representing migrants, including Ruth Philips, who says fees run in the $12,000 range, about twice what her clients in land-border-crossing cases often pay to be smuggled in vehicles.)

Boat crews do not see all the money — a network bears other costs, including fuel and two-cycle oil, and paying for temporary housing for migrants on either side of the border and crews who meet drenched passengers on shore and hurry them from the beach. Some networks, Levan says, also underwrite intelligence operations, including assigning English speakers to review court documents of smugglers brought to prosecution for details of law-enforcement tactics, or managing spotters and their communications around San Diego. They also pay cartel fees for operating on cartel turf. But with per-passenger rates often exceeding $10,000, a panga with 10 or 15 migrants can generate more money in one night than a pair of small-boat fishermen might see in a year, a fact that makes pangas — inexpensive skiffs with old engines worth a few thousand dollars — practically and financially disposable, the plastic spoons of the smuggling world.

Pangas are not the only means of reaching California by water. Smugglers sometimes use personal watercraft like Jet Skis to ferry single passengers, dumping them near land and reversing the journey alone. Fast and maneuverable, these craft frustrate most interdictions. In fiscal 2020, smugglers used personal watercraft at least 88 times near San Diego, according to law-enforcement data. Smugglers also operate stolen pleasure boats, hiding migrants in cabins to blend into traffic. One agent said distinguishing stolen boats from legal boats is less like looking for a needle in a haystack than "looking for a needle in a stack of needles." As sensor operators have become adept at spotting pangas, the smugglers' use of pleasure craft has increased.

C.B.P.'s refit with new aircraft and vessels over the last decade, coupled with smuggler persistence, have pitted two sides in risky open-water matchups. With four outboard engines delivering a combined 1,400 horsepower, Coastal Interceptor Vessels can reach speeds exceeding 65 miles per hour, faster than any panga yet encountered in California waters. This means agents frequently overtake smuggling boats and order them to stop.

Many smugglers comply, yielding to the imposing arrival of an enforcement boat with blue lights flashing. Some smuggling crews drive on, trying to beeline or outmaneuver pursuers long enough to reach either the surf or legal sanctuary in Mexican waters. Lawyers who represent migrants say that because smugglers face harsher legal treatment than passengers, when a panga is detected, the interests of smugglers and migrants can instantly diverge — in situations in which migrants are vulnerable and powerless. "It is not uncommon for load drivers, whether in a car or on a boat, to try to avoid apprehension at all costs," Philips says. "Our clients get hurt when it ends badly." She adds, of the drivers: "I would compare them to mules, who don't worry about the safety or comfort of their cargo and will discard them if and when necessary to evade arrest."

When smuggling vessels flee, agents follow a set of practiced escalations they call the "small-boat interdiction program." This begins with an agent firing a pair of red flares from a Remington 870 12-gauge shotgun, typically across a noncompliant vessel's bow. If the boat does not stop, the Interceptor pulls alongside and the agent fires with disintegrating frangible ammunition into the boat's engine. Frangible ammunition, designed to be nonpenetrating, is less likely than a solid slug or bullet to ricochet off an engine block; the C.B.P. says it reduces chances of harm to people in pangas and that stopping vessels this way is safer than allowing overloaded boats to reach the surf, where migrants have drowned. Shotgun blasts from about 10 feet at engines that panga drivers often hold by tiller are intimidating to the point of being psychologically overpowering. They tend to bring chases to an end. But smuggling captains' skills and intentions vary, and boats sometimes collide. In 2012 a panga rammed an inflatable Coast Guard boat near Santa Cruz Island, killing Senior Chief Petty Officer Terrell Horne III. In 2015 a panga and an enforcement vessel collided, and the panga capsized, pitching 20 migrants into the water and leading to the drowning of Graciela Lopez Franco, a 32-year-old citizen of Mexico. A federal judge found the accident "was solely caused by the erratic operation of the panga by the driver." Robert Schroth, a lawyer who represents migrants, said passengers that night pleaded with the panga driver to stop, but he was reckless and high on meth.

Even without the perils of high-speed, low-light interdiction, California's big surf and cool waters claim lives. Passengers leaping from small craft for short swims to shore have drowned, including a man whose body washed up at La Jolla in 2017. On occasion pangas swamp or roll over, pitching people into waves or rip currents, as happened last August when two migrants died at Ocean Beach. Wheat, the defense attorney, surfs early most mornings. By chance he arrived soon after this incident and saw the two men dead on the sand near gathering Border Patrol agents.

The wind was down and seas were glassy one night in October 2019 when a Coast Guard cutter spotted a skiff crossing from Mexican waters. The boat was moving fast — 38 knots, the first radio chatter said – almost 44 miles per hour. This was faster than the cutter. The sensors on an aircraft overhead showed a boat packed with people, about a dozen in all. Two Interceptor vessels rushed from their piers. Aluminum hulls rose up as they accelerated through the channel, climbing to a speed of 57 knots, about 65 miles per hour. They wove past kelp beds south of Point Loma and into the open Pacific.

The panga had a 20-mile lead, which put math in its favor: The enforcement vessels would need an hour at full throttle to pull alongside. In that time the panga could pass roughly 40 miles of beaches, onto almost any of which it could drop passengers. But the smugglers had been seen, so they also faced a movable gantlet on land. From a flight-operations center at North Island, Supervisory Air Interdiction Agent Christopher Cokeley, a former Air Force F-16 pilot, radioed updates. Cokeley is regarded by colleagues as especially attentive to data; he has combed through records and reports in search of patterns and tried to adjust C.B.P. patrol times to what the data says about smuggler habits and tactics. In this dash the agents knew the panga captain probably had an intended landing spot, where waiting guides and rides would be positioned to usher migrants from surf to freeway, then to stash houses in San Diego or Orange Counties. Border Patrol agents were preparing to cut them off and round them up on foot.

Running parallel to shore, the chase reached a long patch of near darkness at the Marine Corps base at Camp Pendleton, then the bright lights of the Border Patrol checkpoint on Interstate 5. The panga — on a straight compass heading — had traveled far enough to be closer to Los Angeles than San Diego. When enforcement boats were minutes behind, Cokeley's voice again came over the radio. At the operations center, he was watching a live sensor feed. The driver had turned east toward San Clemente. The skiff rode through the surf north of the Trestles, a popular point break. Passengers spilled out. "He's on the beach!" Cokeley said. "He's on the beach!"

Agents on the ground arrived. "They're running north toward the train tracks," Cokeley said. Inland and uphill the migrants climbed, across the tracks, over a steep bank to a grove of towering palms, rushing onto the palatial grounds of a waterfront mansion during their first minutes in the United States. Cokeley consulted a street map and called out the address. The C.B.P. boats bobbed just outside the surf, watching Border Patrol agents fan out with flashlights. One by one, they began running the passengers down. Soon they detained six citizens of China and three of Mexico. At least two people eluded capture; their nationalities remain unknown.

High-speed dashes are not the only way. Some migrants forgo boats and fees altogether. They swim, wading from beaches in Tijuana, stroking out to sea and crossing the border away from land. Then they turn east, guided by the skyline glow, and slip ashore near Imperial Beach — feats of endurance and athleticism requiring hours in chilly water at night. Infrared video cameras on shore, watched from a Coast Guard operations center, often detect their efforts. Enforcement boats are then sent out. When swimmers are struggling or ask for assistance, agents pull them aboard and hand them off to Border Patrol in the harbor. This has costs. Ferrying swimmers takes an Interceptor off the water for hours. Some agents said they suspect smugglers send swimmers to tie up enforcement assets, then run pangas or personal watercraft across the line. In fiscal 2020, the authorities documented 97 "swimmer events" in these waters, a record; in the last year of the Obama administration, there were 24.

C.B.P. agents transferring migrants to the enforcement vessel, with the smugglers handcuffed at the stern.

The night after the panga landed in San Clemente, the Coast Guard alerted agents on a graveyard shift that swimmers had been spotted on video crossing the line. Bundled in watch caps and jackets, the agents started engines, headed to water off Imperial Beach and began puttering through darkness, blue lights flashing and white searchlight sweeping the surface. Marine Interdiction Agents Evan Wagley and Craig Jenkins stood at gunwales and peered into the night. Wagley, a former Border Patrol agent who captains fishing charters, spends more time on the water than perhaps any of his peers; during this week he had worked grueling hours, chasing tuna by day and patrolling for pangas at night. He was on the long chase to San Clemente the night before and now carried himself against the 1:45 a.m. chill with a moonlighter's measured pace.

The seas were without swell, and the sky was moonless. The polluted Tijuana River leaves Mexico and drains through an estuary on the American side. A cold wind blew from shore. Even more than a mile out, the ocean smelled of sewage. The boats slid slowly through wind and stink. The searchlight fell upon a pair of heads and shoulders rising above the water. Two swimmers were side by side, squinting into the light. One was an adult man, the other appeared to be a teenager, possibly his son. They were more than a mile inside U.S. waters and a similar distance from shore in water about 30 feet deep. The ocean temperature was in the low 60s. They wore wet suits but no fins. The younger swimmer had looped his right arm through an inner tube the size of a wheelbarrow tire, a makeshift life ring. From it a small plastic bag dangled in the water; such bundles typically contain personal items — dry clothes, a phone, money, a bit of food — bare provisions to start life in the United States.

The pair kept swimming. Jenkins dropped a yellow life preserver onto the water beside them. They paid it no mind. "Agua," the older man said. Jenkins tossed him a plastic bottle of water. The swimmers turned vertical, treaded water and shared it. When they finished, the empty bottle floated away as they stretched themselves horizontally and swam away from the boat again. The vessels followed behind. Truck lights flashed on shore where Border Patrol agents waited. Agents told the swimmers to head to the light and make a decision. If they stepped onto dry sand they would be detained. If they remained in the water, even knee-deep, they could walk back to Tijuana without arrest.

The interaction was typical of law-enforcement encounters with migrants on the water: limited to the point of glancing. Agents rarely learn migrants' names, much less anything of their background. They pass them to land-based agents. These swimmers were a Border Patrol case now. The vessels spun and headed back to sea. The swimmers, they later heard, opted to trudge back to Mexico.

Calm weather persisted for several nights, creating conditions in which agents expected more smugglers to risk runs. Many of the same agents were on duty a few nights later when an aircraft crew spotted a panga loitering near the Coronado Islands. This was the Lazora. It was loaded with people a few miles south of the line, positioned for a run. J. was aboard.

The panga's crew, agents said, was probably making phone calls, asking spotters whether C.B.P. boats were at their docks or calling drivers to ensure passengers would be met with rides. At about 12:45 a.m. two C.B.P. vessels left the harbor. They drove fast, navigation lights out to avoid being seen, beyond a point where they thought the panga might cross. They settled into an idle about 10 miles west-southwest from Point Loma, seven miles north of the border. They were in several hundred feet of water, inside the Coronado Escarpment, where the bottom falls away clifflike and the sea floor is more than a half-mile down. They waited.

To their south the Lazora lingered. For an hour, Cokeley, the supervisory agent, shared its compass headings and speeds. The panga stopped, started, steered erratically, stopped again. "Target heading 250 at 12 knots," he said. The boat was driving west, away from land. Agents suspected its crew knew an aircraft was circling.

At 2 a.m. the Lazora slowed again. At 2:47 Cokeley declared it "D.I.W." — dead in the water, no longer making way. Nautical twilight was about three hours off. If the smugglers planned to put their passengers ashore before Southern California woke, time was short. At 2:56 a.m., the sensor showed it: The Lazora had turned toward American waters. It was heading north at 20 knots.

At this heading and speed, the panga would leave Mexican territory in about 15 minutes. An agent said the last pause may have been the panga captain's final check. "He probably made a phone call," he said, "and they said, 'Go!'" The Lazora accelerated to 24 knots, crossed the line and turned east. "They are starting to head to Point Loma," Cokeley called out.

At about 3:15 a.m., agents throttled engines and closed in. The pursuit was swift. The lead boat approached the Lazora's port stern and switched on lights. The panga pressed on. In the bow, Marine Interdiction Agent Kurt Nagel, a former Marine Corps machine-gunner, fired two shotgun flares about five seconds apart. They flew past the panga and landed on the water. Nagel pumped the shotgun and chambered the first frangible round. The driver kept fleeing. The enforcement vessel pulled in close. From about a dozen feet away, Nagel fired into the outboard engine, then again. The impacts struck about two feet from the smuggler at the tiller. The Lazora stopped.

It was a cheerless sight: a white-and-blue trimmed panga, packed with people, engine cowling showing holes where shotgun rounds hit. Cold and deflated, the passengers barely spoke. A few women clustered in the middle. Men huddled forward and aft, including one whose torso was clothed in only a short-sleeved T-shirt. J. was among them. Nagel and Wagley stepped on board, handcuffed the men at the engine and leaned them forward onto their chests.

The man in short sleeves bent over the Lazora's starboard gunwale and vomited red fluid. "Careful," Wagley said. "Tuberculosis." Another agent wondered if the passenger was wounded. The migrant managed the wan smile of a seasick man. "No, no," he said. "Jugo," Spanish for juice. He nodded to an empty juice container sloshing in the panga's bilge.

In 35 min

utes it was over. One C.B.P. boat steamed away, carrying detainees for processing. The crew of the second C.B.P. boat fastened a rope to the Lazora's bow and began towing. It would be impounded, then shredded — the end of one panga in a fleet that keeps coming.

On Oct. 31, 2019, the two men running the Lazora, Juan Audelo-Guerra and Adan Audelo-Medina, were charged with federal crimes: bringing in aliens for financial gain, and bringing in aliens without presentation, punishable by prison sentences as long as 10 years.

The passengers faced less legal peril but considerable hardship. Classified as material witnesses, they were deemed necessary if the Audelo cases went to trial. They were indefinitely detained, held in legal limbo in prisonlike conditions at the San Luis Regional Detention Center in Arizona. This practice, common under the Trump administration, frustrated many lawyers for migrants, who call it punitive, inhumane, unnecessary and expensive to taxpayers. Under previous administrations, they said, the government often released migrants on bail, and many were able to work temporarily or go home.

In the Lazora case, the government freed the witnesses and returned them to Mexico by early 2020, when the smugglers opted for plea agreements. Juan Audelo-Guerra, who admitted to captaining the Lazora, was sentenced to 24 months' imprisonment; Adan Audelo-Medina, the refueler, received 13 months and a day.

J. had anticipated wading ashore in California before a sunrise in October, paying his fee and being reunited with his family in November. From the outset his journey brought disappointment. On the night he and his fellow passengers met the Lazora, he saw only a few life preservers. The coyotes had lied. He boarded nonetheless and rode north, into fresh legal trouble. Again, his fingerprints revealed his identity and immigration record, which showed that when he tried to re-enter the United States on the Lazora he remained under supervised release for the 2018 misuse-of-documents case. The judge who sentenced him in that case now ordered him to serve six more months in jail.

J. spent late 2019 and the first months of 2020 in the Western Region Detention Facility in San Diego, a private prison, where he was visited occasionally by Wheat. The prison is blocks from where vessels that detained him dock, and throughout his incarceration the C.B.P. was busy. Smuggling boats kept crossing, sometimes tragically. A few weeks after his arrest a boat carrying 13 people in foul weather capsized in Mexican waters, killing nine. In February 2020, the engine on a panga stalled while approaching Imperial Beach. The driver, previously convicted of smuggling, dove into the water, abandoning his passengers to the fate of a boat adrift. The panga flipped. Two migrants drowned. Last fall the driver was sentenced to 83 months' imprisonment for trying to smuggle in illegal migrants resulting in death, and other charges.

While J. served his sentence, his stepdaughter traveled to San Diego to visit him. They had not seen each other in two years. When guards brought him out, she was shocked. Before her was her family's patriarch, jailed for trying to reach home. He looked weak, tired and frail. His diabetes, she says, was untreated. "He lost so much weight," she says. He avoided looking her in the eyes.

During the trip, aching for real reunion, wondering if J. would ever live with his family again, his stepdaughter visited La Jolla, the point jutting into the Pacific about 10 miles north from where J. had hoped to land.

A watery vista spread before her — an area where many nights pangas try to pass and where in 2017 a migrant washed up dead. Racked with sorrow, she allowed herself to dream. She almost thought she could see him out there, somehow evading the patrols, drawing near. "I was looking at the ocean," she says. "I was envisioning him finally coming home."

GREAT AMERICA

Great America, in my opinion, is a collection of the ideas we share about freedom, equality, justice and benign government. It should not be defined as a barrier to make a secure border.

Much of the historical data cited herein comes from Wikipedia, courtesy of the internet. My opinions were also informed by several wonderful books including *1491* by Charles Mann and *Abundance* by Peter Diamandis.

Immigration has been steady in the years since 1900 except when it plummeted during the great depression when xenophobic laws reduced the numbers. Some think the laws passed made our economy worse. As a percentage of population, the number of immigrants were much higher in the 16th and 17th centuries when we had tremendous growth and innovation.

Major laws passed include *The Chinese Exclusion Act of 1882* which was repealed in 1943. The Equalization act of 1924 was meant to keep out Jews, Italians and Slavs. The Justice Department's *Operation Wet Back in* 1954 disrupted the lives of millions.

On a brighter note, *The Immigration Equalization act of 1965*, sponsored by Ted Kennedy brought a bit of sanity to an insane system. It focused on reuniting families and attracting skilled labor from abroad.

Some 65,000,000 immigrants have come to our sacred land since 1900. They are well represented in industry, the armed forces, education and government. They have made America great.

I like to think that immigrants bring more than weary bodies and downtrodden souls. They also bring minds, new ideas, colorful customs, and energy.

Consider the poor people coming across the southern borders on foot. Their ancestors built colossal cities and empires before fateful 1492. Their forebearers were astronomers and mathematicians, agronomists and more. We are still eating their corn and potatoes – crops which the early Europeans had no knowledge. The original inhabitants of the Americas were defeated by disease and relegated to the trash heap of American history.

Pick a number… any number of minds. Give them an environment free of fear want, and threat. Stand back and see what they can accomplish. Great science, great societies, and great achievements in all endeavors will result. Look what America has done. America was created by migrants from the beginning.

It is with these ideas that I say, "To hell with Trump's stupid wall idea! Throw open the gates. Build bridges. Help all who come to our borders."

And what should we do with the dreamers — those eight-million minds already here? Those valedictorians, future physicians and generals?

We can and should import more minds. A mind, you know, is a terrible thing to turn away.

RUMINATIONS

WHAT MOVES ME
Environmental Factors

Daisy, my beloved spouse – there's no doubt she is the most critical 'Mover' in my universe. We spend a lot of time together, often in companionable silence, always aware of each other's moods and desires. I go to great lengths to please her. I am not always successful.

The New York Times – I believe that the NYT is the world's best newspaper. With 1500 reporters trying to get to the truth of the matters covered, they provide a great deal of information every morning

Reading – besides reading newspapers every morning, my consumption of books has informed my life for many, many years.

Television – Yeah, we watch it a lot. CNN. CBS. BBC. Streaming services for entertainment. Probably more than sane people should.

My **Publishing work** – Research and Conversations. I learn so much every day that I have a tough time remembering the lessons. Dontcha just love Google?

A **long memory** of past events and travels – Man, oh man. I keep rerunning reels of the thousands of interactions with sharp people and things from even fifty and eighty years ago.

Corporal clues – my body talks to me every day. It tells me what I can and can't do.

Imagination – When past events are not enough. I make things up in my reveries and dreams.

~ ~ ~

Thinking about this essay has encouraged me in the belief that I have lived many lives.

I have been a child growing into a young man in the special neighborhood of Flatbush in Brooklyn. I was a teenager in Farmingdale, on Long Island, New York. And, for a decade, a starving student at both Hofstra College and the University of Miami.

Suitor, married man, father, divorcé, devoted husband, and grandfather were favorite roles.

~ ~ ~

In adulthood, work has often been life's defining factor. If you ask me, "What do you do?" I'll often replied with what I did for a living. Ask me now and I'll say, "I'm a writer and a publisher."

Work can be fun. I was a sailor in the U.S. Coast Guard. As a reservist, I served for over 30 years and wound with the rank of commander. I had the privilege of serving as the commanding officer of two Coast Guard reserve units for half a decade. The Coast Guard now provides me with a pension and many benefits.

I've worked as a bowling alley pinsetter, a nurseryman, a forester, a janitor, a courier, a banker, and then a medical administrator.

Unemployment has struck more than once. That was okay, but experiences as a restaurant owner, a restaurant shift manager, a serial entrepreneur, a cook, a waiter, a sous chef, a salesman, and a newspaper publisher were better.

I signed up as Uber driver at eighty and segued that work into an airport transportation business. At eighty-two-years of age I retired from transportation. I am still a competent driver, but I figured that it would be better to quit while I was ahead, knowing that I must stop driving when old age demands.

Working as an author and a publisher of books for others is my current fun.

Traveling the world from Asia to the Middle East, Europe, Australia, Africa, New Zealand. Pacific Islands. South America, Alaska, the Caribbean and more has enriched life for Daisy and me. I have experienced many good things and now, as an octogenarian, still enjoy living and have fun working.

What moves you?

MY RUDDER

I cannot say that I have had a reliable compass course for living my life. My parents didn't give me a lot of formal guidance, although eight years of Sunday School gave me a strong Christian input into how one should behave. All of that occurred in the Dutch Reformed churches in Brooklyn, New York.

Perhaps avoidance of conflict is one of my driving principles. Yes. I think I largely owe that to the sibling rivalry with my older sister in my formative years. She always won.

The phrase, "**A dance with luck, relying on unplanned encounters and unfolding episodes...**" somehow resonates with me and describes much of my life.

So, now as an old man, approaching my sunset, you might say that love of man and love of life are in the driver' seat. I cringe at the war news and stories of hunger, crime and poverty that come every day.

If I were King of America, I'd renounce war. To this end I'd sponsor the establishment of a strong multinational court, under the United Nations umbrella, to enforce a ban on armed conflict between nations. This supposes a continuing reliance on international trade for all nations. Loss of the ability to buy from and sell to other countries would be punishing.

My America would have a much-reduced budget for military matters and a higher budget for social programs, giving priority to universal health care, education, and elimination of poverty. In my country, people would be free to start and engage in businesses as they please. Taxes would be fair. I would try to be more like Gandhi than the 'Prince of the World.'

Working in jeans and a tee shirt would suit me. I'd only wear a tie on frigid winter days. I'd ensure that the office of king would revert to our traditional democracy in five years and live off the royalties from the book every ex-king should write.

"So," you ask. "Why bring all this up?" and, "What guides you now?"

My answer would go something like this. "I have been blessed with long life and still have some gas left in my tank.

"My dance with luck has left me in a comfortable place where I can observe the world and marvel over the technology that gives me a warm shower every morn and a cool place to rest at the end of each day. Anything I need or want, including groceries and medications, will arrive at my doorstep in short order. My several physicians keep a careful watch on all my systems.

"I am easily able to scribble essays and memoirs using my Iphone and MiniMac's Microsoft Word for Mac. My collections of writings are easily formed into books that can be bought worldwide. And into digital books too. They'll be available for years beyond my last breath.

And to cap it off I am able to publish books for others, at a modest price, that will help others leave footprints in the sands of time.

What A Way To Go!

MY FRIEND

My friend, Father Time, stops by every few days. His purpose is to remind me that my time on earth is soon to expire. Neither of us knows my expiration date. So, we just chat a bit and wish each other well.

I might say something like, "I'm feeling fine and think that I might last for years longer and get to see how events turn out. I hope, and try to believe, that things on earth will improve for all mankind. What do you think?"

Father Time plays it close to his chest. "Willie, my boy. I wish all my customers were optimistic like you. Most of them don't let me in. They don't want to talk at all. "I'll see you again. Soon."

He leaves so quietly. I'm pretty sure no one else in the family has seen him at all.

Feeling good is something I seek. It consists of being pain-free, not being criticized for my behavior or performance, and believing that I am purpose-driven to shout out to all in my world that they are valued and will be given equal opportunities.

Feeling down can be a function of age as we realize our declining capabilities. No more mountains to climb, no more batons to grasp in the race, and no more grand ambitions. But I still have a few 'irons in the fire' that pull me up every morning.

WRITING – I am a member of two small writing workshops that meet regularly. The members struggle to present new fiction, poetry, memoirs, and essays every week. So, there are deadlines to meet and that is the source of the work in *Light songs*

PUBLISHING – Getting into a profession that wasn't quite realized during work years is a blessing. In my case, I have learned how to take a manuscript and turn it into a real paper book, available on Amazon, and into a Kindle eBook, and to share this skill with others.

I have published eleven books under my name and even more for others.

Publishing is fun and it has kept me busy. I try to keep the costs down. You can have a look at my books at billserle.com

The work is done in my home office. There was no great cost or investment in my little business. I just use my desktop computers and the services of trusted vendors for art and printing.

The thing I can't do for my clients is to sell their work – they must do that themselves. The goal is to make beautiful books and I have found a small measure of success.

Here's a partial list of titles that I have published.

BY WILLIAM SERLE ~
Stealing Ali
Hunter I
Hunter II
Hunter III
The Hunter Trilogy (Kindle only)
Grandfather Uber
The Chiming of Forgotten Bells
Swaying in the Wind
Light Songs We Breathe
Bill's Journey (Website only – billserle.com)
Gammy (Website only)
Edna's Love Letters (Website only)
Fred's Gold (Screenplay – Website only)

BY OTHERS ~
She Who Laughs, Lasts – Karen Slotta
Haiti: The Living Pearl – Beverly Grondin
Kickapoo Kronicles – Rick Wright
Tai Chi Diary – Rivka Sappington
The Adventures of Grant and Duncan –
        Jay Kuppel Genauer and Rivka Sappington
Rockledge Writers Workshop – Annual Anthologies (4)
Scribblers of Brevard – Annual Anthologies (3)
Word Magic – Ormond Beach Writers Workshop
        Anthology
Heirloom Recipes – Spade & Trowel Garden Club
Kitt's Kronicles – Kitt Haney
Moos and Mischief – Paula Mae Taylor
Here and There, Then and Now – Paul Hill
Generations of Women – Ina Dean-Masters

The services I offer to clients usually include formatting their work into a book, creating a cover, inserting the table of contents, and other elements such as title pages, ISBN codes, and other forward essentials. The manuscripts are grammar and spell-checked by my Microsoft Word application. Both digital and paper proofs are created then I work with the author to correct formatting and copy problems.

Finally, when all is satisfactory, the book will be offered for sale by Amazon both as a paperback book and on Kindle as a digital edition.

It is done at a modest cost. Typically, for a 350-page book, I'll spend about ten hours formatting and doing the above, and perhaps another hour working on the cover. I charge $50.00 per hour. (Friends $35.00 per hour. Family $65.00 per hour. Works of love are free of charge) A proof might cost less than $5.00 for printing plus sales tax and postage. Probably less than $15.00 total.

So it goes. Let's all bear down and try to make the best use of our time allotments. **Perhaps we'll leave some footprints in the Sands of Time.**

Oops! Stand by. Father time is at the door.

IN THE ZONE

I confess to a smallish comfort zone for most of my life. Perhaps limited to my home and family. The ultimate example was my private hot tub garden behind our Rockledge, Florida home. At night, alone, under moon and stars, *au naturale*, I would laze away a spell *sans* television and telephones, and dream about life as Bill.

Thinking about the title-notion, I realized that many of the best things in my life occurred when I stepped out of my comfort zone. In addition to building personal confidence and wealth, I expanded my comfort zone to embrace most of humankind and the earth we inhabit. I'll give you a few examples – snippets of my life follow:

Evelyn Soper ~ Being a shy kid, I was overshadowed by my brilliant blond sister and, because of my size, older playmates who did everything better than yours truly. Goaded by a friend, I invited Evelyn to go on a double-date and then the senior prom. Our friendship lasted two years and I learned to relate to the opposite sex in a respectful way. She never once hit me.

United States Coast Guard Reserve ~ Dirt poor and working three jobs, the University of Miami kicked me out because I fell behind on my tuition payments. I enlisted to fulfill my military obligation in lieu of being drafted. I learned that there was robust life outside of school. This became a 30-year side-career and I retired as a commander.

First National Bank of Miami ~ I applied for a job and was told, "No openings." I went back to the bank every week for a month until they said yes. Thus began an eight-year banking stint that taught me a ton about business and led to being recruited by…

Siegal Medical Group ~ I stayed with Doctor Siegal for 18 years, and learned a lot more about how business can work upwards and downwards. There I met and married the fabulous Daisy Alonso.

Toastmasters and an Effective Speaking Class ~ Oops. I forgot to mention that the Bank offered professional training through the American Bankers Association. Still shy, I took a class called Effective Speaking, mistakenly believing that it would work on conversational skills. I thought I'd die when it turned out to be about public speaking, i.e., giving speeches. But I suddenly found I had the ability to enjoy public speaking. I joined Toastmasters. My comfort zone exploded. I became a teacher and a leader in the Coast Guard and beyond.

Terrace Café ~ When the love affair with Doctor Siegal ended, Daisy and I set out to go into business for ourselves. It worked brilliantly. We had no capital, so I set out to sell shares in a limited partnership to finance a restaurant. I learned several things: • I was a good salesman.

• Owning a business can be the path to ruin.

• Retreat can be a valuable tool.

Nantahala Outdoor Center ~ Daisy and I reinvented ourselves during two-score-plus years of sojouring in the mountains of western North Carolina. We labored for this outdoor recreation company (rafting, mountain climbing, fly fishing etc.) for eight years. We prospered. She eventually became a valued employee and leader at Harrah's Cherokee Casino. I entreprenured my way into the publishing business.

Fun Things To Do In The Mountains ~ I founded and ran this tourist guide and for 14 years – I often think of this time as the best period of my life, using everything learned in the years before – always way, way out of my comfort zone, continually learning and using new skills.

Uber and the Airport Transport Business ~ I take a little pride that I began these adventures around the age of eighty. I got material for a little book, *Grandfather Uber,* met a lot of good people and augmented our already-sufficient retirement income.

The Old Ormond Beach Superior Poker Club ~ Yea, even though I am retired, I need the company of friends. Reverting to an early childhood understanding that smoking cigarettes, drinking whisky, and playing poker was the way adults have fun. I tried to find a game but, after a few futile months, decided to start my own society of poker friends.

Again, outside of my current comfort zone, I was rewarded by success. I have over a dozen new pals to play with every Friday afternoon and now, even on Wednesdays. Alas, no ciggy butts or whisky.

Ormond Beach Writers Workshop ~ Believe it or not friends, joining a group to comment on my writing was a bit of a tiptoe outside of my zone.

I'm glad stepped out from time to time. I was often rewarded and now feel happy and confident just about anywhere. I love learning new things.

¿Quiere aprender Español ahora?

MY POKER PALS

I grew up in Brooklyn, New York. My parents played poker with Aunt Betty and Uncle Dick Wilhelm. Some of early memories include standing by the table and watching the adults have fun. I loved the clink of ice in highballs, the haze of cigarette smoke, the flapping of cards being shuffled, and the clatter of poker chips as bets were made and pots raked in by winners. I was finally allowed to play at about eleven.

So, poker is my idea of adult fun.

***

Daisy and I moved to Rockledge, Florida from Allamuchy, New Jersey in 2010. I didn't play my favorite game for the ten years we enjoyed in our new Florida home.

I missed the New Jersey poker buddies who played in a condo game room. We were a bunch of old folks. At 72 years old, I was a relative youth.

This Jersey group loved poker, and each other, but they acted tough. They yelled at each other and at me – always willing to complain and chastise when they felt any breach of poker protocol or personal etiquette. Being from Brooklyn, I was used to their guttural New Yorker accents.

"Bill!"

"What, Arlene?" I snarled back.

"You're a goddamned sandbagger. That's not fair. When you have a good hand, you must bet. No fair sneaking up like that."

"Whadda ya mean? I've been watching *World Series of Poker*, and that's how you should bet. I was using my poker face," I explained as I raked in my half of the pot.

She grumbled, but she let me slide a little since she'd just won the other half of the chips.

Milton was not feeling so calm. As Bernie dealt the next hand, Ray, the Italian guy, reached out

Clockwise from the bottom.

Ray: Tough kid from Italy. WWII. U.S. Army vet, writing a book. Bossy. Fun!
George: Jersey boy loves poker and his buds. Talks loud with sign language. Bossy. Fun!
Bossy. Fun!
Milton: Kindly Montclair, New Jersey antique store owner. Table's senior citizen. Bossy. Fun!
Bernie: My neighborly friend. Cards three times a week. Philosopher card shark. Bossy. Fun!
Bill: Sandbagger. Talks too much. Needs supervision. Having fun!
Arlene: Poker Queen. Weekly bus trips to Atlantic City hotels and casinos. Bossy. Fun!
Empty chair: Probably took the photo. Likely bossy.

and arranged some cards around the table a little as they weren't flying so straight. "Take your hands off my fucking cards!" Milton shouted at him as he reached out and put a little restraining hand on Anthony's arm.

George was losing. "Bill! This is all your fault," he said, "Don't mess around. You talk too much. Keep your mind on the game." He correctly sensed that I was confused, as usual, and didn't quite get the game that had been called. "Rows and columns. Rows and columns, *nuttin* wild."

His fingers waggled in my face, signaling forefinger for the rows, index finger for columns, and a thumb-forefinger circle for *nuttin* wild.

For the years I participated, we never played stud, Texas hold-'em, or draw poker. We played strange, ever-changing games called *Bingo, Two Plus Two Plus One, Tic Tack Toe, Red and Black, Rows and Columns, Morris' Pea Patch,* and such. Always high and low. Brands of poker that were fun but not strictly kosher in my book.

I'd win occasionally, but usually, when I drifted home after midnight and Daisy asked, "How'd you do?" I'd have to say, "I had a lot of fun." Code for losing my shirt.

Well, not really. We played for nickels and dimes, and, on my worst night, I'd lose about $25.00. Now and again, I might even win a little.

I loved that this gang cared about the game enough to argue and squabble. Sometimes one of them would disappear for a few weeks due to some imagined or real affront.

Bernie Salinger was a neighbor, so we carpooled to the game. Our conversations during the half hour it took each way were wide-ranging. They ran the gamut from philosophy to finance to family and life experiences. I usually drove since Bernie didn't see well at night. We took turns as to whose car we drove. Daisy and I became good friends with Bernie and his wife, Patricia. Dinners at each other's homes or restaurant outings were equal fun. I miss my New Jersey friends.

***

We sold our home in Rockledge in early 2018 and moved to our present home – a beautiful bungalow that we remodeled into a home suitable for an older couple. A paradise. It's on my son Jeff's property in Flagler Beach. We are sited with a stunning front-door view of Florida's prettiest pool, and, from the deck, we see Bulow Creek.

Growing older, I searched for worthwhile activities. I joined the Ormond Writers Workshop and a book club. I gave up bicycling and sailing my lovely little skiff. I started a business providing airport transportation to Orlando, Jacksonville, Sanford, Daytona, and even far-off Miami. I gave that work up on my 82nd birthday. I am still a competent driver but who knows for how long?

***

Some five years ago I began asking friends and neighbors if they'd like to play poker. No dice.

Down, but not defeated, I advertised on the NextDoor app and was able to round up enough players to start a Friday afternoon game at the Ormond Beach Senior Center. *Ooh oh happy days…*

I now have 17 names in my phone's 'Poker' contacts list, and we have been playing on a regular basis and have spawned other games on other days.

The cast is dedicated to playing by the rules of poker etiquette. Except for highballs and cigarettes, the banter is much the same as in my boyhood memories.

Ormond Beach, Florida

Clockwise from the bottom,

Lloyd: Poker parliamentarian.
Bill: Banker and host. Designated loser.
Ann: Our Baker,
John. Master of the game.
Carol Lynn: Jolly, kind, and beautiful.
John II: Retired army.
Everett: The bingo caller.
Joshua: Having fun.

Joshua reminds me of my young self, Billy, who loved to hang out around his parent's game.

PUBLISHING

There was a time that I got into the business of transporting clients to area airports including Orlando MCO, Orlando/Sanford FBS, Daytona DAY, and Jacksonville, JAX. I also took people to doctor appointments and, occasionally, as far afield as Miami's cruise port.

It was better money than Uber and I got to know some of my regular clients. I even published a book for one. (*Kick a poo Kronicles*)

I decided to quit the business on my 82nd birthday. I was, and still am, able to drive the distances but I know that the day will come when I cannot drive safely. I wanted to quit *before* that day.

My next step was to offer my services to clients who want to independently publish their work.

I am still doing publishing work for clients.

MY MIGRANT
SUPER-POWER

In the day-to-day cycle of existence, I accomplish nutrition, keeping things sanitary, doing laundry, shopping, housekeeping, and a hundred other important domestic things, major and minor, with an absolute minimum of effort.

"How," you might ask, "can you do so much with little effort?"

The answer is simple. "I have a Super-Power. Her name is Daisy. We take care of each other. But she, my dear wife and life's companion, clearly does more for me than I do for her."

There have been so many emotional moments in my life, including the birth and death of dear ones. She is always there, and I'm a better man because of her steadying influence.

The joys of traveling the world, the simple delights of dining out, enjoying television, or attending a great theatre, are magnified by her presence. We have much to talk about, yet we are often content in companionable silence.

She communicates so well. In two languages. And her nonverbal signals are always strong.

Sometimes a little grunt or "a-hum" will tell me what she wants or what's bugging her.

If I am lucky enough to win at poker or to take a good photo with my iPhone, I can't wait to share it with her. My rewards for these occasions are thusly multiplied.

I greet all present when walking into a room for the first time with a pleasant word and, if there are more than a few folks there, at least make eye contact and a head bob. Daisy, however, lights up such a room. I don't know how she does it, but all I need to do is follow her in and smile. She'll own the room!

Family relationships are better with Daisy aboard. She makes birthday phone calls and 'Just to say hi,' calls on a regular basis. Grandchildren, nieces, and nephews call her on *my* birthday!

Daisy has kind regard for all humanity and is quick to forgive, even when *I* offend. Migrants have a special place in her heart as she emigrated from Cuba as a girl and learned the English language the hard way – in school, one conversation at a time, and by watching TV.

So, dear Reader, salute Daisy with me. Our world is a far better place with you on board.

ODE TO MY SUPERPOWER

Oh, Daisy Pooh!
I Love you.

Give me a hug
So's I don't have to bug

You now or later.
Tell me what I can do

To soothe the hurt
That seems to lurk

Just outta sight,
A little to the right

Of Adolph and Benito
And in the wheelhouse

Of the Orange Man*
Who says only *he* can

Save us from ruin
And marauding refugees soon

To replace white men
At the podium.

Let's not vote
With little feet.

Let's speak out and shout
"We are a nation of refugees!"

And here's a nod to all
Not just the pale and tall.

We're glad you're here
And have no fear

Because we need you to
Put shoulder to the wheel,

All fears to rest
And mind to the test.
                    *President Donald Trump

This illustration evokes thoughts of birds
settling at sunset in the tidal wetlands around
our home in Flagler County, Florida.

ABOUT BILL

Je Maintiendrai

William Serle is a retired U.S. Coast Guard Reserve commander and publisher. He has written four novels, three biographies and four books of essays and poetry. He has edited and published numerous books and literary anthologies for others.

Visit billserle.com.